To Nicole,
happy Valentine
Day
Love Grandma

Crochet WITH One Sheepish Girl

Easy Lessons & Sweet Designs for
Wearing, Living & Giving

Meredith Crawford
onesheepishgirl.com

sixth&spring
books
NEW YORK

sixth&spring books

161 Avenue of the Americas, New York, NY 10013
sixthandspringbooks.com

Library of Congress Cataloging-in-Publication Data
Crawford, Meredith.
Crochet with one sheepish girl : easy lessons and sweet designs for wearing, living & giving / Meredith Crawford, onesheepishgirl.com.
    pages cm
ISBN 978-1-936096-78-7 (paperback)
1. Crocheting—Patterns. I. Title.
TT825.C734 2014
746.43'4—dc23
                              2014006107

Manufactured in China

1 3 5 7 9 10 8 6 4 2

First Edition

EDITORIAL DIRECTOR
JOY AQUILINO

MANAGING EDITOR
KRISTY MCGOWAN

DEVELOPMENTAL EDITOR
LISA SILVERMAN

ART DIRECTOR
DIANE LAMPHRON

YARN EDITORS
CHRISTINA BEHNKE
VANESSA PUTT

EDITORIAL ASSISTANT
JOHANNA LEVY

SUPERVISING PATTERNS EDITOR
LORI STEINBERG

PATTERNS EDITOR
PAT HARSTE

PAGE DESIGN
ARETA BUK

PROOFREADER
ERIN SLONAKER

PHOTOGRAPHER
KELLY CHRISTINE MUSGRAVES

FASHION STYLIST
MEREDITH CRAWFORD

HAIR
POUF BLOWOUT SALON

MAKEUP
CHANTAL HICKMAN

VICE PRESIDENT
TRISHA MALCOLM

PUBLISHER
CAROLINE KILMER

PRODUCTION MANAGER
DAVID JOINNIDES

PRESIDENT
ART JOINNIDES

CHAIRMAN
JAY STEIN

Contents

Introduction 7

GETTING HOOKED 8

WEARING 28

LIVING 50

GIVING 94

Facts & Figures 122

Resources 125

Acknowledgments 127

Index 128

Granny Square Infinity Cowl
page 30

Color Block Ribbed Turban
page 34

Bow Brooch
page 36

Striped Bow Clutch
page 38

Sweater Makeover
page 42

Collared Shirt Makeover
page 45

Scallop Stripe Cowl
page 48

"Home Cozy Home" Pillow Case
page 52

Crochet Edge Frames
page 57

Heart Pocket Apron
page 72

Teacup Coasters
page 76

"Enjoy" Place Setting Placemat
page 79

Gift Boxes
page 96

Crochet Latte
page 104

Blueberry Muffin
page 107

Yarn Bag Makeover
page 60

Ombré Baskets in Three Sizes
page 62

Crochet Hook Organizer
page 66

Cottage Tea Cozy
page 84

Diana Camera Purse
page 88

Tablet Case
page 91

Party Hat Garland
page 110

Snow Cone Garland
page 113

Crochet Edge Cards and Tags
page 116

Introduction

When I started my blog, One Sheepish Girl, in August 2010, it was a way for me to use crochet to express my creativity. From the moment I hooked my first stitch, my hands were constantly busy with an endless stream of crochet teacups, granny squares, and afghans.

While I was crocheting up a storm, without even realizing it I was also coming out of the shell of shyness I'd lived in my entire life. The "quiet girl" label had stuck with me all the way through college, and I figured it would be impossible to escape. Who knew the combination of blogging and crochet would banish that persona forever! I never expected a colorful ball of yarn to be a source of confidence, joy, and imagination. My love of blogging and yarn has taught me that confidence isn't a volume, loud or quiet. Confidence is a feeling that comes from doing something you are passionate about, even something as small as an unexpected trip to a craft store on a random Sunday afternoon.

One Sheepish Girl is my place to feel free to explore my creativity and connect with other yarn-loving people around the world. Crochet is a beautiful art form, and I feel so blessed to be able to share my inspirations and ideas with you!

This is the book I wish I'd been able to read after I first learned to crochet. It's filled with contemporary projects perfect for wearing, living, and giving—you'll see that crochet is not limited to blankets and hats! And the techniques within these pages are fit for beginners and experienced crocheters alike. If you love to wield a crochet hook, you will find something fun and inspiring to create, along with step-by-step photo tutorials for everything from the basic stitches to more advanced (and unique!) techniques.

With its stylish photos, beautiful illustrations, project inspirations, tips, tricks, and more, I hope this book stirs the same creative passion in your life that it has in mine.

Enjoy and be confident with your creativity!

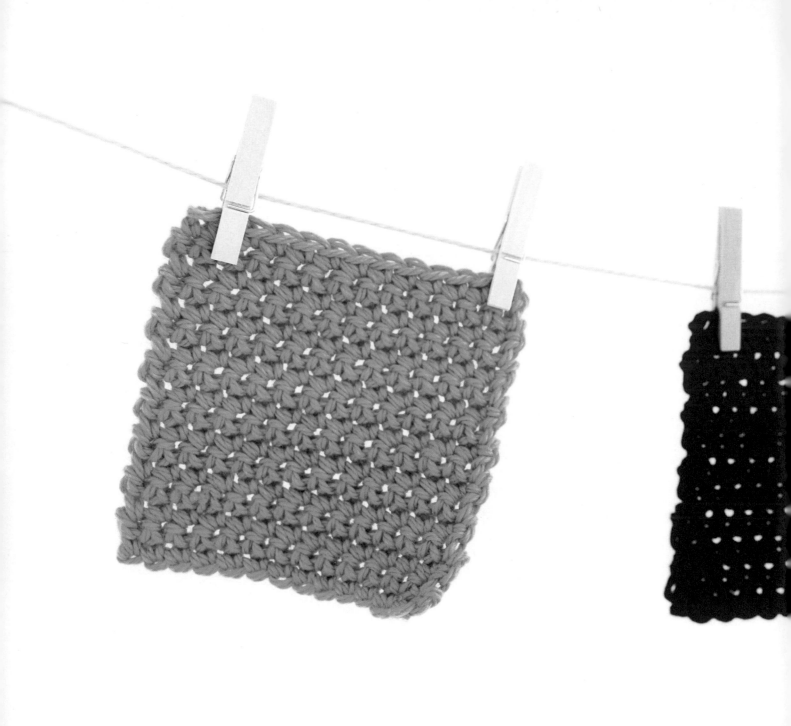

Getting Hooked

Materials and Tools ..... page 10

Basic Crochet Stitches ..... page 13

Embroidering Chain Stitch on Crochet ..... page 20

French Knot ..... page 22

Sewing a Zipper on Crochet ..... page 23

Spray Blocking Crochet ..... page 24

Tablet Case Lining ..... page 25

Diana Camera Purse Fabric Lining ..... page 26

Crochet Edge Cards and Tags ..... page 27

Materials and Tools

Before you dive into the world of crochet, get familiar with the tools of the trade. Simply fill your yarn bag with hooks, scissors, a notebook, and yarn, yarn, yarn. Once you get your hands on the materials, it's time to get started! Even your yarn bag can be a quick and easy project—see page 60 for a way to spice up an old tote.

Choose the best yarn for both your project and your wallet. Get some balls of wool, cotton, acrylic, and blends and try them out to see what you like best.

Crochet hooks come in different materials. Choose what feels best in your hand and what works best with the yarn for your project. You might want to use a metal needle with wool yarn—metal is smooth and fast and wool yarn is grabby, which makes for slower going. A bamboo hook will be a bit slower, so you might want to use it with a slick yarn, such as a mercerized cotton, for a bit more control. Plastic hooks are good with all yarns, and they are easy on your hands.

Everyone should have the following tools in his/her crochet bag of tricks:

Stitch markers

Stitch markers are used for marking the beginning of a round of crochet or on any stitch that requires attention.

Scissors

A small pair of scissors is necessary for finishing projects and snipping excess yarn after weaving in the ends.

Tapestry needle

When you finish a crochet project, a large, blunt tapestry needle is perfect for weaving in the ends of yarn or for sewing seams.

Measuring tape

Keep a measuring tape handy to measure your gauge and the lengths of the pieces as you're stitching.

Notebook

Designate a notebook strictly for crochet notes, doodles, and designs. Keep track of the number of stitches and the current round of your project, or jot down ideas for a new pattern!

Find or create a spot to store your crochet tools, so everything you need will be in one place.

Basic Crochet Stitches

The basic stitches are the foundation for endless crochet possibilities! You can create hundreds of projects with just the beginning techniques.

SLIP KNOT

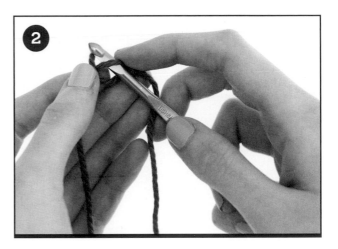

With the yarn in your left hand and the crochet hook in your right hand, make a loop of yarn, leaving a tail about 6 inches/15 centimeters long at the end. With the end of the yarn attached to the ball, make a second loop behind the first loop.

Place the hook inside the second loop and draw it through the first loop.

Pull the ends of the yarn to tighten the slip knot on the crochet hook.

FOUNDATION CHAIN

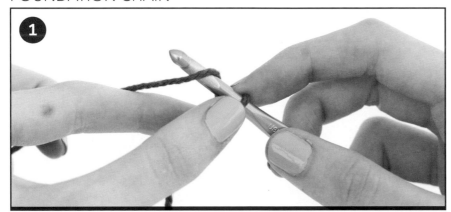

Make a slip knot and position it close to the end of the hook. Wrap the end of the yarn attached to the ball around the hook. To do this, bring the yarn up from behind and over the hook from right to left. This is called "yarn over."

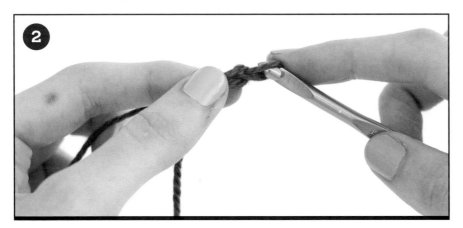

Next, draw the yarn through the loop on your crochet hook by using the hook to pull it toward you.

You just made one chain stitch! Pull the yarn to tighten if the chain is loose, or wiggle the hook to loosen the chain if it is tight. Repeat these steps to make the number of chains listed in the pattern. Make each chain the same size. Count the number of chains by holding the chains vertically so each stitch resembles the letter "V." Do not count the loop on the hook or the first slip knot. Once you have the correct number of chain stitches, you are ready to start your project!

SINGLE CROCHET (SC)

Insert the hook under both the front and back loops of the "V" in the second chain from the hook, or under the loops of the stitch in the previous row. Yarn over (by wrapping the yarn behind and over the hook from left to right) and catch it with the hook, as shown.

Draw the yarn through the chain or stitch.

Now you have two loops on the hook. Yarn over again …

and draw the yarn through the two loops.

One single crochet stitch is complete! Continue across the chain or the row by inserting the hook into each chain or stitch in the row and repeating the above steps.

When you reach the end of the row, chain 1 and turn your crochet so the loop is at the beginning of the row. You are now working on the "wrong side" of the crochet piece. To start the next row, insert the hook under both loops of the first stitch, skipping the chain stitch, and repeat the single crochet steps across the row.

DOUBLE CROCHET (DC)

Yarn over and insert the hook under both loops of the stitch in the previous row.

Yarn over again and draw the yarn through the stitch.

Now you have three loops on your hook. Yarn over and draw the yarn through the first two loops.

Now you have two loops on the hook.

Yarn over and draw the yarn through the remaining two loops to complete the double crochet.
Repeat these steps across until you reach the end of the row. To start the next row, chain three stitches and turn.

HALF DOUBLE CROCHET (HDC)

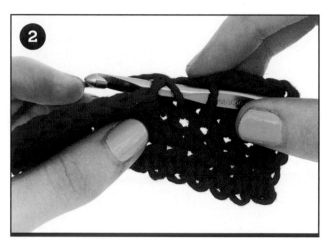

Yarn over and insert the hook under both loops of the third chain stitch from the hook or the designated stitch in the previous row.

Yarn over again and draw the yarn through the stitch.

You now have three loops on the hook.

Yarn over and draw the yarn through all three loops. One half double crochet stitch is complete! Repeat these steps until you reach the end of the row. To start the next row, chain two stitches and turn.

TREBLE CROCHET (TR)

Yarn over twice and insert the hook in the designated stitch in the previous row.

Yarn over again and draw the yarn through the stitch.

You now have four loops on the hook. Yarn over and draw through the first two loops on the hook.

Now three loops remain on the hook. Yarn over and draw through the next two loops.

Now two loops remain on the hook. Yarn over and draw through the last two loops.

One treble crochet stitch is complete! Repeat these steps across until you reach the end of the row. To start the next row, chain four stitches and turn.

SLIP STITCH (SL ST)

Insert the hook in the stitch indicated in the pattern.
Yarn over and draw through both the stitch and the loop on the hook.
One slip stitch is complete. This stitch is mainly used for joining circles and shaping pieces.

SECURING THE LAST STITCH (FASTENING OFF)

When you reach the end of your project, cut the yarn, leaving a 6-inch tail. Pull the tail through the last loop with the crochet hook. Pull the tail tightly until the loop is secured around the yarn tail.

WEAVING IN THE ENDS

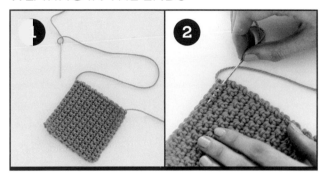

Thread the yarn tail through the eye of a tapestry needle. Starting in one direction, bring the needle through the top of the stitches close to the edge and on the wrong side of your crochet piece.

Next, bring the needle back in the opposite direction, piercing the top of the yarn. This will anchor the yarn tail in the stitches. To finish, cut the yarn tail as close to the stitches as possible. Stretch the crochet fabric so the yarn tail will disappear inside the stitches.

CHANGING COLORS

To change colors, crochet in the first color all the way to the second-to-last stitch.
Begin the final stitch as usual in the old color until you reach the final yarn over. Take your second color and draw it through the last two stitches on your hook.

Chain the appropriate number of stitches and begin the next row in the new color.

Embroidering Chain Stitch on Crochet

Trace the design you want to embroider on a piece of tracing paper. Make sure to use a dark ink or pencil so it will be easy to see against the crochet fabric you are embroidering.

Cut around the design, leaving a 1-inch border for pinning. Place the tracing paper exactly where you want the embroidered design. Measure if necessary to ensure the proper position. Pin the tracing paper to the crochet with straight pins, as shown. Double and triple check that the design is exactly where you want it!

Cut a long length of yarn and thread the tapestry needle. Tie a knot about an inch from the end. Starting at the first point of the design, bring the yarn through the back of the crochet and up through the tracing paper, letting the knot sit loosely on the wrong side of the crochet fabric. The paper will tear when you pull the needle and yarn through.

Insert the needle down through the same place where you just pulled the needle up, and then up again to the right side where you want the next stitch to begin. You can use your thumb to gently hold the yarn in place as you form the stitch.

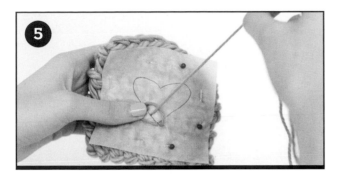

Pull the yarn through gently to form the loop around the strand, as shown.

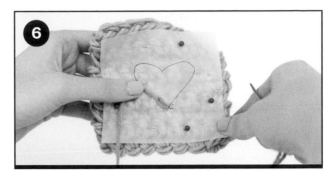

As each chain is done, hold the yarn along the outline to determine where you want the next stitch to begin.

Keep a similar tension for all of your stitches for a uniform look. Bring the needle down through the same point and repeat the chain stitch until the design is complete.

If you run out of yarn, simply cut and knot a new length and pick up where you left off.

When you finish embroidering the design, gently tear the tracing paper away from the design. Untie the knots and weave the ends into the wrong side of the crochet fabric.

French Knot

Thread a tapestry needle with a length of yarn. Pull the yarn up through the crochet fabric from the wrong side to the right side, as shown.

Holding the needle approximately 2 inches/5 centimeters above the crochet fabric, wrap the yarn around the needle twice from back to front, as shown.

Holding the yarn behind the needle, keep the thread tight and insert the point of the needle into the fabric close to the point where the yarn is coming out of the fabric. Push the wraps gently down the needle, close to the surface of the fabric.

Draw the yarn through to the wrong side to complete the French knot.

Sewing a Zipper on Crochet

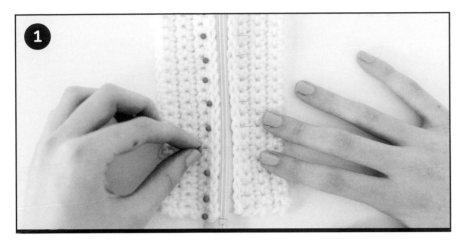

Lay the zipper flat. Place the crochet piece over the zipper so that the ends of the zipper are flush with the ends of where you want the opening in the crochet piece, and the edges of the crochet fabric are close to the zipper teeth—but not so close that the fabric is likely to get caught in the zipper. Pin the zipper in place using straight pins and being sure to keep the crochet fabric flat, so it doesn't pucker between the pins.

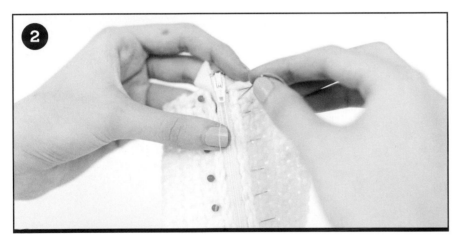

Using a sewing needle and thread that matches the yarn and the zipper tape, secure the zipper in place with a back stitch at the bottom of the opening. With the right side facing you, sew a straight line along the column of crochet stitches at the edge of the opening. Back stitch at the top of the zipper tape and sew the other side of the zipper along the opposite edge of the opening.

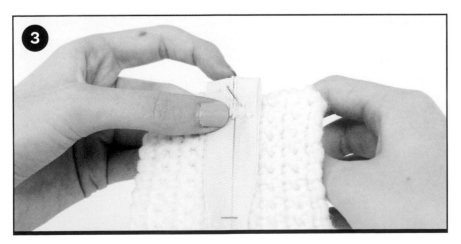

Fold the excess zipper tape at the top and the bottom of the opening to the wrong side of the zipper, as shown, and sew it in place to secure.

Spray Blocking Crochet

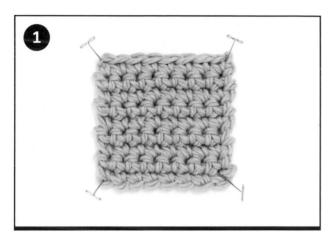

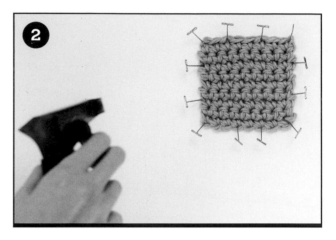

Lay the piece to be blocked on a blocking board or on a piece of white foam core board.

Note the specific measurements of the finished item. Use a measuring tape or a ruler and mark the key points on the blocking surface with pins.

With rustproof T-pins, pin the piece to the measurements at the key points. On the square swatch shown, the points are at the corners.

Place pins evenly around the edges of the piece. Continue pinning until the edges are flat.

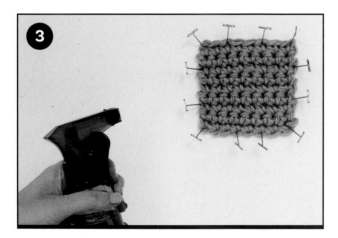

Spray the piece evenly with room-temperature water from a spray bottle.

Leave the pins in place until the piece is dry. You might need to leave the piece pinned overnight. Remove the pins when you are sure the piece is completely dry.

Tablet Case Lining

Turn the tablet case inside out.

Measure from seam to seam across the tablet case and add a half inch. This is the width, plus seam allowance. Measure from the top of the front of the tablet case to the bottom. Multiply by 2 (to include the back of the case) and add 1 inch/2 centimeters for a seam allowance. This is the length.

Mark the lining material for length and width including seam allowances and cut the material in one piece.

Fold ¼"/1cm seam allowance to the wrong side of the material at each edge and iron the fold to hold it in place. Fold the material in half with the right sides together, being sure that the short edges (top and bottom) are even. Pin along the side edges and sew the 2 seams. Turn the lining right side out so that the seams are on the inside. Keeping the tablet case inside out, slip the lining over the case, as shown. The wrong side of the lining is facing the wrong side of the tablet case.

Sew the lining to the upper edge of the tablet opening, as in the photo, and continue around to the back, keeping the lining edge even.

Diana Camera Purse Fabric Lining

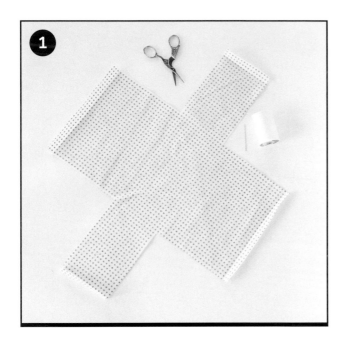

Make a template out of paper as follows:
Measure the base of the purse and draw a rectangle to these measurements at the center of the paper.
Measure the side of the purse and add a half-inch seam allowance to each long side and to the top edge.
Using the short edge of the base rectangle as the center of the short edge of each side, draw a rectangle on each side of the base rectangle. There is now one long rectangle with the sides slightly wider than the center.
Measure the front of the purse and add a half-inch seam allowance to each long side and to the top edge.
Draw a rectangle for the front on each long side of the base.
Cut out the paper along the outer edges of the drawing. The paper template is the shape of a plus sign. Pin the lining material to the template and cut it out.

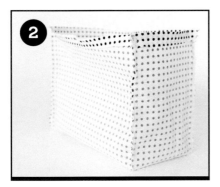

Fold the edges of the material one half inch to the wrong side and iron the folds to hold them in place.
Form a corner in the lining as follows: With the right sides together, hold the upper edge of the front of the lining together with the upper edge of one side of the lining. Keeping the upper edges even, pin along the edge to the bottom. Sew the seam. Repeat for the remaining three corners.

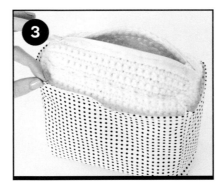

Turn the purse inside out. Turn the lining right side out and place the purse inside the lining. The wrong sides of the purse and the lining are together.

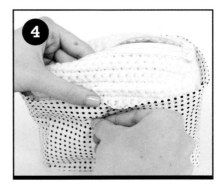

Sew the lining around the top edge and down the corner edges to attach it to the purse.

Crochet Edge Cards and Tags

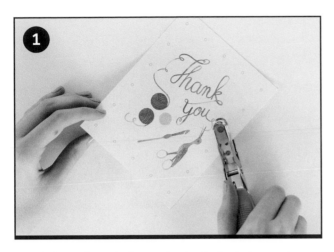

Punch through each dot marked with the hole punch. Hold the card still and punch firmly to get a clean hole.

After joining the yarn through the first hole with a slip stitch, chain 3 and work a slip stitch through the next hole. If you are working with a lighter weight yarn, you might need more chains between each hole. If you are working with a heavier yarn, you might need fewer chains between each hole. Be sure to chain the same number each time to keep the look even.

Continue to work along the edge of the card in this way until you have worked a slip stitch in the first corner.

Chain 3 (or your desired number of chains) and join with a slip stitch in the same corner hole, as shown. Continue around until you have worked into each punched hole.

Granny Square
Infinity Cowl
30
·
Color Block
Ribbed Turban
34
·
Bow Brooch
36
·
Striped Bow
Clutch
38

Sweater
Makeover
42
·
Collared Shirt
Makeover
45
·
Scallop Stripe
Cowl
48

wearing

Granny Square Infinity Cowl

Granny squares have traditionally been used to make beautiful afghans. I decided to play with tradition and create this snuggly soft cowl, to bring the coziness of an afghan with me wherever I go! The leaning tower stitch creates a densely textured fabric.

FINISHED DIMENSIONS
GRANNY SQUARE
10" x 10"/25.5cm x 25.5cm
COWL
Circumference 59"/150cm
Width 10½"/26.5cm

HOW TO MAKE AN ADJUSTABLE RING

1) To begin, wrap the yarn loosely around 2 fingers, with the loose tail near your fingertips and the working yarn to the inside.

2) With the crochet hook, bring the working strand under the outside strand, then draw a loop through.

3) Draw through another loop to complete the single crochet. When all the stitches called for have been worked into the ring, close the ring by pulling the loose tail.

STITCH GLOSSARY
Edc (Extended double crochet)
Yo, insert hook into the space indicated and draw up a loop, yo and draw through first loop on the hook (this forms a chain stitch at the base of this stitch), [yarn over and draw through two loops on hook] twice.

LTS (Leaning Tower Stitch) Work an Edc in the space indicated, *yo, insert the hook through the center of the chain stitch at the base of the Edc, [yo and draw through 2 loops on hook] twice; rep from * once more—2 dc worked in an Edc.

PLTS (Partial Leaning Tower Stitch) Work an Edc in the space indicated, yo, insert the hook through the center of the chain stitch at the base of the Edc, [yo and draw through 2 loops on hook] twice—1 dc worked in an Edc.

YARN
Rialto DK by Debbie Bliss, 1¾oz/50g, each approx 115yd/105m (extra fine superwash merino wool); DK weight

• 3 balls in #52 Lavender (E)

• 2 balls each in #44 Aqua (B), #20 Teal (C), #51 Indigo (D), and #04 Grey (F)

• 1 ball in #09 Apple (A)

HOOK
• Size H/8 (5mm) crochet hook *or size to obtain gauge*

GAUGE
4 rnds = 4" x 4"/ 10cm x 10cm square over granny square motif using size H/8 (5mm) hook.

To wear,
twist the cowl
around your head
and secure it
under your
neck.

Granny Square Infinity Cowl

GRANNY SQUARE MOTIF (MAKE 6)
With color A, make an adjustable ring.
Rnd 1 (RS) Ch 3 (always counts as 1 dc), work 11 dc in the ring, tighten the ring, join rnd with a sl st in top of ch-3—12 dc.
Rnd 2 Ch 3, work PLTS between last dc made and beg ch-3 of rnd below, [skip next 3 dc, work 2 LTS between next 2 dc] 3 times, end skip next 3 dc, work LTS between last dc and ch-3 of rnd below, join rnd with a sl st in beg ch-3—4 corners made. Fasten off.
Rnd 3 With right side facing, join B with a sl st between beg PLTS and last LTS of rnd below. Ch 3, work PLTS in same space as joining, *LTS between next 2 LTS, work 2 LTS between 2 LTS; rep from * around twice more, end [LTS between next 2 LTS] twice, work LTS in same space as beg PLTS, join rnd with a sl st in top of beg ch-3.
Rnd 4 Ch 3, work PLTS in space between beg PLTS and last LTS of rnd below, *[LTS between next 2 LTS] twice, work 2 LTS between next 2 LTS; rep from * around twice more, end work LTS between next 2 LTS, work LTS in same space as beg PLTS, join rnd with a sl st in top of beg ch-3. Fasten off.
Rnd 5 With right side facing, join C with a sl st between beg PLTS and last LTS of rnd below. Ch 3, work PLTS in same space as joining, *[LTS between next 2 LTS] 3 times, work 2 LTS between next 2 LTS; rep from * around

twice more, end [LTS between next 2 LTS] 3 times, work LTS in same space as beg PLTS, join rnd with a sl st in top of beg ch-3.
Rnd 6 Ch 3, work PLTS in space between beg PLTS and last LTS of rnd below, *[LTS between next 2 LTS] 4 times, work 2 LTS between next 2 LTS; rep from * around twice more, end [LTS between next 2 LTS] 4 times, work LTS in same space as beg PLTS, join rnd with a sl st in top of beg ch-3. Fasten off.
Rnd 7 With right side facing, join D with a sl st between beg PLTS and last LTS of rnd below. Ch 3, work PLTS in same space as joining, *[LTS between next 2 LTS] 5 times, work 2 LTS between next 2 LTS; rep from * around twice more, end [LTS between next 2 LTS] 5 times, work LTS in same space as beg PLTS, join rnd with a sl st in top of beg ch-3.
Rnd 8 Ch 3, work PLTS in space between beg PLTS and last LTS of rnd below, *[LTS between next 2 LTS] 6 times, work 2 LTS between next 2 LTS; rep from * around twice more, end [LTS between next 2 LTS] 6 times, work LTS in same space as beg PLTS, join rnd with a sl st in top of beg ch-3. Fasten off.
Rnd 9 With right side facing, join E with a sl st between beg PLTS and last LTS of rnd below. Ch 3, work PLTS in same space as joining, *[LTS between next 2 LTS] 7 times, work 2 LTS

between next 2 LTS; rep from * around twice more, end [LTS between next 2 LTS] 7 times, work LTS in same space as beg PLTS, join rnd with a sl st in top of beg ch-3.
Rnd 10 Ch 3, work PLTS in space between beg PLTS and last LTS of rnd below, *[LTS between next 2 LTS] 8 times, work 2 LTS between next 2 LTS; rep from * around twice more, end [LTS between next 2 LTS] 8 times, work LTS in same space as beg PLTS, join rnd with a sl st in top of beg ch-3. Fasten off.
Rnd 11 With right side facing, join F with a sl st between beg PLTS and last LTS of rnd below. Ch 1, sc in same space as joining, sc in each rem st around, join rnd with a sl st in first sc. Fasten off, leaving a long tail for sewing. Weave in all other ends.

ASSEMBLY
1) Block squares to finished dimensions.
2) With the right sides facing, whipstitch the squares together through the back loops. Turn the cowl right side out.

EDGING
With the right side facing, join color F in the corner of any granny square.
Rnd 1 (RS) Ch 2, hdc in each sc around, join rnd with a sl st in top of ch-2. Fasten off. Weave in the end. Repeat around opposite edge. ■

Color Block Ribbed Turban

For me, a gray winter day is no reason to hide my love of color. This headband takes two trends, color blocking and turbans, and combines them in one bold accessory! Front and back post stitches create the unique ribbed texture.

FINISHED DIMENSIONS
Circumference 22"/56cm
Width 4½"/11.5cm

STITCH GLOSSARY
FPdc (Front Post double crochet)
Yo, insert hook from front to back around the post of the next st of the row below, yo and draw up a loop, [yo and draw through 2 loops on the hook] twice.
BPdc (Back Post double crochet)
Yo, insert hook from back to front around the post of the next st of the row below, yo and draw up a loop, [yo and draw through 2 loops on the hook] twice.

TURBAN
STRIP A
With color A, ch 13. Work in dc rib pat as follows:
Foundation row Dc in the 4th ch from the hook and in each ch across. Turn.
Row 1 (RS) Ch 3 (counts as 1 dc), skip the first dc, *FPdc around the next st of the row below, dc in the next st; rep from * to the last st, end FPdc around next st of the row below, dc in top of t-ch. Turn.
Row 2 Ch 3 (counts as 1 dc), skip the first dc, *BPdc around the next st of the row below, dc in the next dc; rep from * to the last st, end BPdc around next st of the row below, dc in top of t-ch. Turn.

Rep rows 1 and 2 until the piece measures 24½"/62cm from beg (about 59 rows). Fasten off, leaving a long tail for sewing.

STRIP B
With color B, ch 13. Work as for strip A.

ASSEMBLY
1) Fold strip A in half with the wrong sides facing.
2) Place the folded strip on the work surface, so the folded end is at the bottom.
3) Lift up the top layer of the strip, then flip the top edge of the bottom layer over to the left, so the right side is now facing up. Place the top layer on top of the bottom layer, so the top and side edges are even.
4) Using a long tail, whip stitch the top edges together. Weave in the ends and snip the excess.
5) Thread strip B through the loop of strip A. Fold in half with the wrong sides facing. Repeat steps 2–4.
6) With the right sides facing, whip stitch the top edges of strips A and B together, forming the turban. Weave in the ends and snip the excess. ■

YARN
Sweater by Spud & Chloë, 3½oz/100g, each approx 160yd/146m (superwash wool/organic cotton); worsted weight

• 1 hank each in #7513 Jelly Bean (A) and #7518 Barn (B)

HOOK
• Size H/8 (5mm) crochet hook *or size to obtain gauge*

NOTIONS
• Straight pins

GAUGE
16 sts and 10 rows = 4"/10cm over dc rib pat using size H/8 (5mm) hook.

Try using subtle neutrals for a different take on color blocking!

Bow Brooch

Top off your favorite coat with a pretty bow! This quick craft comes together with a few simple stitches and twists. Use up your scrap yarn pieces and make a rainbow of brooches. String a handful together to make a bow garland, or replace the safety pin with a barrette and wear this colorful crochet bow in your hair!

YARN
Cotton DK by Debbie Bliss, 1¾oz/50g, each approx 92yd/84m (cotton); DK weight

• 1 ball in #13058 Indian Pink

HOOK
• Size G/6 (4mm) crochet hook

NOTIONS
• Small safety pins

• Straight pins

GAUGE
Gauge is not important for this project.

FINISHED DIMENSIONS
Width 1¼"/3cm
Length 3¼"/8cm

BOW
LONG STRIP
Ch 30.
Row 1 Sc in the 2nd ch from the hook and in each ch across—29 sc. Turn.
Row 2 Ch 1, sc in each sc across. Fasten off, leaving a long tail for sewing.

SHORT STRIP
Ch 10.
Row 1 Sc in the 2nd ch from the hook and in each ch across—9 sc. Turn.
Row 2 Ch 1, sc in each sc across. Fasten off, leaving a long tail for sewing.

ASSEMBLY
1) Measure and mark center of long strip with a straight pin.
2) Hold the center of the strip between your left index finger and thumb.
3) To make the first loop, *use right index finger and thumb to bring the top edge of the strip over and around to the back. Now twist the end to the left and bring the end to the center of the strip*. Pin end in place with another straight pin; remove straight pin from center.
4) To make the second loop, turn the strip so the opposite end is at the top. Repeat from * to *, butting this end with the first end. Pin end in place.
5) Using the long tail, sew the ends together and to the center of the strip. This side is the front of the bow. Weave in the ends and snip the excess.
6) Wrap the short strip around the middle, so ends are at the back of the bow.
7) Using the long tail, sew ends of strip together and to the center of the bow. Weave in the ends and snip the excess.
8) Pin a safety pin on the back of the bow. ■

Attach your new brooch to your favorite coat, purse, or anything that needs a bit of flair!

Striped Bow Clutch

Take this classy clutch with you on a fancy night out. It was inspired by a beautiful dress that also had a bold black-and-white stripe design and was topped off with a graphic bow. I love incorporating fashion trends in my crochet designs!

FINISHED DIMENSIONS
CLUTCH
Width 8¾"/22cm
Height 6½"/16.5cm
BOW
Width 2¾"/5.5cm
Length 4½"/11.5cm

NOTE
When changing colors, draw new color through last 2 loops on hook to complete last st, then turn.

STITCH GLOSSARY
sc2tog [Insert hook in next sc, yo and draw up a loop] twice, yo and draw through all 3 loops on hook.

BACK
With color A, ch 35.
Row 1 (RS) Sc in 2nd ch from hook and in each ch across—34 sc. Turn.
Rows 2 and 3 Ch 1, sc in each sc across. Turn.
Row 4 Ch 1, sc in each sc across, changing to A. Turn.
Row 5 Ch 1, working through back loops only, sc in each sc across. Turn.
Rows 6 and 7 Ch 1, sc in each sc across. Turn.
Row 8 Ch 1, sc in each sc across, changing to B. Turn.

Row 9 Ch 1, working through back loops only, sc in each sc across. Turn.
Rows 10 and 11 Ch 1, sc in each sc across. Turn.
Row 12 Ch 1, sc in each sc across, changing to B. Turn.
Rows 13–28 Rep rows 5–12 twice more.

FLAP
Rows 29–51 Ch 1, sc in each sc across. Turn. Fasten off, leaving a long tail for sewing.

FRONT
Work as for back to row 28; do not change to B on last row. Fasten off, leaving a long tail for sewing.

BACK LINING
With color B, ch 35.
Row 1 (RS) Sc in 2nd ch from hook and in each ch across—34 sc. Turn.
Rows 2–49 Ch 1, sc in each sc across. Turn. Fasten off, leaving a long tail for sewing.

FRONT LINING
With color B, ch 35.
Row 1 (RS) Sc in 2nd ch from hook and in each ch across—34 sc. Turn.
Rows 2–28 Ch 1, sc in each sc across. Turn. Fasten off, leaving a long tail for sewing.

YARN
Rialto DK by Debbie Bliss, 1¾oz/50g, each approx 115yd/105m (extra fine superwash merino wool); DK weight

• 4 balls in #397 Ecru (B)

• 2 balls in #380 Black (A)

HOOK
• Size H/8 (5mm) crochet hook *or size to obtain gauge*

NOTIONS
• Two ½"/13mm nickel magnetic snaps

• Fiberfill

• Straight pins

GAUGE
15 sts and 19 rows = 4"/10cm over sc using size H/8 (5mm) hook.

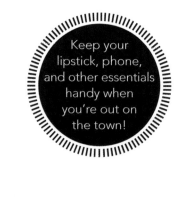

Keep your lipstick, phone, and other essentials handy when you're out on the town!

Striped Bow Clutch

BOW

With color A, ch 3.

Row 1 (RS) Sc in 2nd ch from hook and in each ch across—2 sc. Turn.

Rows 2 and 3 Ch 1, sc in each sc across. Turn.

Row 4 Ch 1, [2 sc in next sc] twice—4 sc. Turn.

Rows 5 and 6 Ch 1, sc in each sc across. Turn.

Row 7 Ch 1, 2 sc in first sc, sc in next 2 sc, 2 sc in last sc—6 sc. Turn.

Row 8 Ch 1, sc in each sc across. Turn.

Row 9 Ch 1, 2 sc in first sc, sc in next 4 sc, 2 sc in last sc—8 sc. Turn.

Rows 10–17 Ch 1, sc in each sc across. Turn.

Row 18 Ch 1, sc2tog, sc in next 4 sc, sc2tog—6 sc. Turn.

Row 19 Ch 1, sc in each sc across. Turn.

Row 20 Ch 1, sc2tog, sc in next 2 sc, sc2tog—4 sc. Turn.

Rows 21 and 22 Ch 1, sc in each sc across. Turn.

Row 23 Ch 1, [sc2tog] twice—2 sc. Turn.

Rows 24 and 25 Ch 1, sc in each sc across. Turn.

Rep rows 2–25. Fasten off, leaving a long tail for sewing.

CENTER WRAP

With color A, ch 4.

Row 1 (RS) Sc in 2nd ch from hook and in each ch across—3 sc. Turn.

Rows 2–9 Ch 1, sc in each sc across. Turn. Fasten off, leaving a long tail for sewing.

MAGNETIC SNAP BACKING (MAKE 4)

With color B, ch 4.

Row 1 (RS) Sc in 2nd ch from hook and in each ch across—3 sc. Turn.

Rows 2 and 3 Ch 1, sc in each sc across. Turn. Fasten off, leaving a long tail for sewing.

ASSEMBLY

1) To make the bow, sew the first row to the last row, forming a circle.

2) Center the seam over the center of the bow, then wrap the center of the bow with the center wrap.

3) Sew the first and last row of the center wrap together, then bring the yarn up through the center of the bow, then back down through the bottom to secure the wrap in place.

4) Sew the side edges of the bow together, stuffing very lightly with fiberfill. Weave in ends. Set aside.

5) Sew the bottom and side edges of the front to the back, matching the stripes. Turn the right side out.

6) Position the bow on the right side of the flap, so the bottom edge of the center wrap of the bow is 1½"/4cm from bottom edge of flap and bow is centered side to side. Sew in place.

7) Sew the bottom and side edges of the front lining to the back lining. Leave wrong side out. Set aside.

8) Attach the magnetic snaps to the crochet backing as per the package instructions.

9) Position the bottom half of each snap on center B stripe on front, so edge of the backing is 1½"/4cm from the side edge of the front; pin in place. Sew backings in place using their tails. Weave in ends. Set the top halves of the snaps aside.

10) Insert the lining.

11) Sew the top edge of the clutch front to the top front edge of the lining, then sew the side and bottom edges of the clutch flap to the lining flap. Weave in ends.

12) Position the top half of each snap on the underside of the flap, so they line up with the bottom halves; pin the backings in place. Snap closed and adjust their positions if necessary. Sew backings in place to the underside of the flap using their tails, taking care not to stitch into the topside (front) of the flap. Weave in ends. ■

Sweater Makeover

As my blog readers know, I am a little sweater-obsessed. Some of my favorites in my ever-growing collection are formerly plain sweaters that I transformed using crochet! This makeover combines ombré crochet hearts and elbow patches to create something truly unique.

FINISHED DIMENSIONS

HEART
Width 1¾"/4.5cm
Length 1½"/4cm

ELBOW PATCH
Width 3½"/9cm
Length 4¾"/12cm

HOW TO MAKE AN ADJUSTABLE RING

1) To begin, wrap the yarn loosely around 2 fingers, the loose tail near your fingertips and the working yarn to the inside.
2) With the crochet hook, bring the working strand under the outside strand, then draw a loop through.
3) Draw through another loop to complete the single crochet. When all the stitches called for have been worked into the ring, close the ring by pulling the loose tail.

STITCH GLOSSARY

sc2tog [Insert hook in next sc, yo and draw up a loop] twice, yo and draw through all 3 loops on hook.

HEART (MAKE 23)

With color A, make an adjustable ring.
Rnd 1 (RS) Ch 4 (counts as 1 tr), working in center of ring, work 2 tr, 3 dc, ch 1, 3 dc, 2 tr, ch 3 (counts as 1 tr), join rnd with a sl st in ring. Tighten the center of the ring. Fasten off. Weave in the ends. Make 8 more using A, and 7 each using B and C.

ELBOW PATCH (MAKE 2)

With color B, ch 7.
Row 1 Sc in the 2nd ch from the hook and in each ch across—6 sc. Turn.
Row 2 Ch 1, work 2 sc in the first sc, sc in the next 4 sc, work 2 sc in the last sc—8 sc. Turn.
Row 3 Ch 1, sc in each sc across. Turn.
Row 4 Ch 1, work 2 sc in the first sc, sc in the next 6 sc, work 2 sc in the last sc—10 sc. Turn.
Row 5 Ch 1, sc in each sc across. Turn.
Row 6 Ch 1, work 2 sc in the first sc, sc in the next 8 sc, work 2 sc in the last sc—12 sc. Turn.
Row 7 Ch 1, sc in each sc across. Turn.
Row 8 Ch 1, work 2 sc in the first sc, sc in the next 10 sc, work 2 sc in the last sc—14 sc. Turn.

YARN
Sweater by Spud & Chloë, 3½oz/100g, each approx 160yd/146m (superwash wool/organic cotton); worsted weight

• 1 hank each in #7513 Jelly Bean (A), #7501 Popsicle (B), and #7518 Barn (C)

HOOK
• Size H/8 (5mm) crochet hook

NOTIONS
• Plain sweater

• DMC 6-Strand Embroidery Floss, 1 skein each in #3607 Light Plum (A), #150 Dusty Rose (B), and #321 Red (C)

• Sewing needle

• Safety pins

GAUGE
Gauge is not important for this project.

Create your own appliqué shapes for uniquely updated sweaters!

Sweater Makeover

Row 22 Ch 1, sc in each sc across. Turn.

Row 23 Ch 1, sc2tog, sc in next 4 sc, sc2tog—6 sc. Turn. Fasten off. Weave in the ends.

ASSEMBLY

1) Lay your sweater out, front side up, on a flat surface. If necessary, you might want to iron the sweater before you begin, so the fabric is smooth. Be sure to check the tag on your sweater before you iron.

2) Evenly space the crocheted hearts on the front of the sweater, with the color A hearts at top and color B and C hearts below. Secure each in place with a safety pin.

3) Using the matching floss, tack each heart in place temporarily with a large up-and-down loop. This will help keep the hearts in place better than the safety pins; remove safety pins as you go.

4) Sew around the edge of each heart with the matching floss. Secure the thread with a knot and snip the excess.

5) Put on the sweater and position the elbow patches over your elbows on the sleeves. Secure the patches in place with safety pins. Take off the sweater.

6) Sew around the edge of the elbow patch with the matching floss. Secure the thread with a knot and snip the excess. Remove the safety pins. ■

Rows 9–16 Ch 1, sc in each sc across. Turn.

Row 17 Ch 1, sc2tog, sc in next 10 sc, sc2tog—12 sc. Turn.

Row 18 Ch 1, sc in each sc across. Turn.

Row 19 Ch 1, sc2tog, sc in next 8 sc, sc2tog—10 sc. Turn.

Row 20 Ch 1, sc in each sc across. Turn.

Row 21 Ch 1, sc2tog, sc in next 6 sc, sc2tog—8 sc. Turn.

Collared Shirt Makeover

Crochet can transform an OK shirt into one that's extra special. This classic contrasting trim starts with a blanket stitch around the collar and down the front. Add a scallop edging and show off your handmade style!

CROCHET THREAD
Fashion Crochet Thread Size 3 by Aunt Lydia's, each approx 150yd/137m (mercerized cotton)

• 2 balls in #12 Black

HOOK
• Size G/6 (4mm) crochet hook

NOTIONS
• Shirt with a peter pan collar

• Large sewing needle

• Water-soluble fabric marking pencil

• Tape measure

GAUGE
Gauge is not important for this project.

PREPARE COLLAR

1) Place the collar on the work surface, so the underside (wrong side) is facing up.

2) Beginning at right-hand edge, use the water-soluble pencil to mark a dot ¼"/5mm from outer edge and just above the topstitched line between the collar and the neckband.

3) Working from right to left, measure and mark the next dot 1"/2.5cm from the first dot and ¼"/5mm from the outer edge. Continue to space the dots at 1"/2.5cm intervals, ending the last dot at the left-hand edge, ¼"/5mm from the outer edge and just above the topstitched line between collar and neckband.

4) Working from the underside of the collar, use the needle to poke a hole in each dot for the pilot holes.

BLANKET STITCH EMBROIDERY

1) Cut a 2½yd/2.25m length of crochet thread.

2) Thread the needle, using the thread doubled. Knot the ends together.

3) With the topside of the collar facing, begin at the left-hand edge of the collar. Working through the pilot holes, and using blanket stitch, embroider the

edge of the collar, ending at the right-hand edge. Secure the end, then cut the thread, leaving a long tail. You will weave in this tail into the crochet edge.

SHELL STITCH EDGING

Make a slip knot and place on the hook. With topside of collar facing, join crochet thread with a sl st under first horizontal strand of the blanket stitch.

Pair with high-waisted shorts or colorful skinny jeans to complete the look!

Collared Shirt Makeover

Row 1 (RS) Work 6 sc in each horizontal thread across. Fasten off, leaving a long tail for weaving in. Make a slip knot and place on the hook. With topside of collar facing, join crochet thread with a sl st in first sc.

Row 2 (RS) Ch 1, sc in same sc as joining, skip 2 sc, work 5 dc in next sc, skip 2 sc, *sc in next sc, skip 2 sc, work 5 dc in next sc, skip 2 sc; rep from *, end sc in last sc. Fasten off, leaving a long tail for weaving in. On underside, weave in all ends. Snip the excess.

PREPARE BUTTON BAND

1) Place the button band on the work surface, so the underside (wrong side) is facing up.

2) Beginning at right-hand edge, use the water-soluble pencil to mark first dot ¼"/5mm from the bottom edge and the outer edge.

3) Working from right to left, measure and mark the next dot 1"/2.5cm from the first dot and ¼"/5mm from the outer edge. Continue to space the dots at 1"/2.5cm intervals, ending the last dot just below the topstitched line between the collar and neckband.

4) Working from the underside of the button band, use the needle to poke a hole in each dot for the pilot holes.

BLANKET STITCH EMBROIDERY

1) Cut a 2½yd/2.25m length of crochet thread.

2) Thread the needle, using the thread doubled. Knot the ends together.

3) With the topside of the button band facing, begin just below the topstitched line between the collar and neckband. Working through the pilot holes, embroider the edge of the button band, ending at the bottom edge. Secure the end, then cut the thread, leaving a long tail. You will weave this tail into the crochet edge.

SINGLE CROCHET EDGING

Make a slip knot and place on the hook. With topside of button band facing, join crochet thread with a sl st under first horizontal strand of the blanket stitch.

Row 1 (RS) Work 6 sc in each horizontal thread across. Fasten off leaving a long tail for weaving in. On underside, weave in all ends. Snip the excess.

PREPARE BUTTONHOLE BAND

1) Place the buttonhole band on the work surface, so the underside (wrong side) is facing up.

2) Beginning at right-hand edge, use the water-soluble pencil to mark first dot ¼"/5mm from the outer edge, just below the topstitched line between the collar and neckband.

3) Working from right to left, measure and mark the next dot 1"/2.5cm from the first dot and ¼"/5mm from the outer edge. Continue to space the dots at 1"/2.5cm intervals, ending the last dot ¼"/5mm from bottom edge.

4) Working from the underside of the buttonhole band, use the needle to poke a hole in each dot for the pilot holes.

BLANKET STITCH EMBROIDERY

Work as for button band.

SINGLE CROCHET EDGING

Work as for button band. ■

Scallop Stripe Cowl

A few years ago I spotted a scallop and stripe combination on an adorable dress fabric, and I knew I had to translate that detail into something crocheted. This bold cowl pattern features color-changing techniques while crocheting in the round.

FINISHED DIMENSIONS
Circumference 23½"/59.5cm
Width 10"/25.5cm

NOTES
1) When changing colors, draw new color through last 2 loops on hook to complete last st.
2) To join yarn with a sc, make a slip knot 5"/12.5cm from end of yarn and place on hook. Insert hook into st, yo and draw up a loop, yo and draw through both loops on hook.

COWL
With color A, ch 48.
Rnd 1 Sc in the 2nd ch from the hook and in each ch across. Then, being careful not to twist this strip, join the strip with a sl st in the first sc, forming a ring.
Rnd 2 Ch 1, sc in same sc as joining (always mark this st to indicate the beg of rnd), sc in each rem st around, join rnd with a sl st in first sc, changing to color B.
Rnd 3 With color B, ch 1, sc in same st as joining, sc in each sc around, join rnd with a sl st in first sc.
Rnd 4 Ch 1, sc in same sc as joining, *skip next 2 sc, work 5 dc in the next sc, skip 2 sc, sc in the next sc; rep from * around, end skip next 2 sc, work 5 dc in

the next sc, skip 2 sc, join rnd with a sl st in first sc, changing to color A.
Rnd 5 With color A, ch 1, sc in same sc as joining, sc in each rem st around, join rnd with a sl st in first sc.
Rnd 6 Ch 1, sc in same sc as joining, sc in each rem st around, join rnd with a sl st in first sc, changing to color B.
Rep rnds 3–6 three times more, then rnd 3 once. Fasten off and weave in ends.

BOTTOM EDGING
With the right side facing, turn the cowl so bottom loops of the beg ch are at top. Join color B with a sc in any loop.
Rnd 1 Sc in each rem bottom loop around, join rnd with a sl st in first sc. Fasten off and weave in ends. ■

YARN
Big Wool by Rowan, 3½oz/100g, each approx 87yd/80m (merino wool); super bulky weight

• 1 ball each in #048 Linen (A) and #063 Lipstick (B)

HOOK
• Size N/15 (10mm) crochet hook *or size to obtain gauge*

NOTIONS
• Removable stitch marker or small safety pin

GAUGE
8 sts and 7 rnds = 4"/10cm over shell st pat using size N/15 (10mm) hook.

Open your mind and draw your own inspiration from fashion and fabrics!

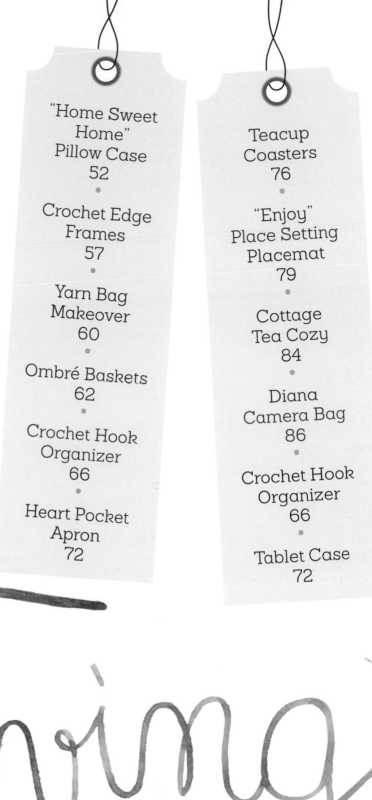

"Home Sweet Home" Pillow Case
52

Crochet Edge Frames
57

Yarn Bag Makeover
60

Ombré Baskets
62

Crochet Hook Organizer
66

Heart Pocket Apron
72

Teacup Coasters
76

"Enjoy" Place Setting Placemat
79

Cottage Tea Cozy
84

Diana Camera Bag
86

Crochet Hook Organizer
66

Tablet Case
72

living

"Home Cozy Home" Pillow Case

Make your home a little cozier with this charming embroidered crochet pillow cover, perfect for your bed or favorite comfy chair.

FINISHED MEASUREMENTS
15" x 15"/38cm x 38cm

STITCH GLOSSARY
sc2tog [Insert hook in next sc, yo and draw up a loop] twice, yo and draw through all 3 loops on hook.

LOWER BACK
With larger hook and MC, ch 29.
Row 1 (RS) Sc in the 2nd ch from the hook and in each ch across—28 sc. Turn.
Rows 2–20 Ch 1, sc in each sc across. Turn. Fasten off and weave in the ends.

UPPER BACK
FLAP
With larger hook and MC, ch 29.
Row 1 (RS) Sc in the 2nd ch from the hook and in each ch across—28 sc. Turn.
Row 2 Ch 1, sc in each sc across. Turn. Fasten off and weave in the ends.
Row (buttonhole) 3 Ch 1, [sc in the next 4 sc, ch 2, skip the next 2 sc] 4 times, sc in the last 4 sc. Turn.
Row 4 Ch 1, [sc in the next 4 sc, work 2 sc in next ch-2 sp] 4 times, sc in the last 4 sc. Turn.
Rows 5–19 Rep row 2. Turn. Fasten off and weave in the ends.

EDGING
With right side facing, turn piece so bottom loops of beginning ch are at top.

With smaller hook and CC, join yarn with a sl st in first bottom loop of beginning ch.
Row 1 (RS) Sc in same loop as joining, sc in each bottom loop across. Fasten off and weave in the ends.

BUTTON (MAKE 4)
With smaller hook and CC, ch 2.
Rnd 1 Work 6 sc in the 2nd ch from the hook. Do not join. Mark the last stitch made with the stitch marker or safety pin. You will be working in a spiral, marking the last stitch made with the stitch marker or safety pin to indicate end of rnd.
Rnd 2 Work 2 sc in each sc around—12 sc. Weave in tail from beginning ch.
Rnd 3 Sc in each sc around.
Rnd 4 [Sc2tog] 6 times, inserting a bone ring before closing opening, join rnd with a sl st in first sc. Fasten off, leaving a long tail for sewing.

FRONT
With larger hook and MC, ch 29.
Row 1 (RS) Sc in the 2nd ch from the hook and in each ch across—28 sc. Turn.
Rows 2–35 Ch 1, sc in each sc across. Turn. Fasten off and weave in the ends.

"HOME COZY HOME" EMBROIDERY
1) Trace each word of the design on page 54 on the tracing paper.
2) Cut out each word separately.

YARN
Outer by Spud & Chloë, 3½oz/100g, each approx 60yd/55m (superwash wool/organic cotton); super bulky weight

- 3 hanks in #7220 Rhino (MC)

Sweater by Spud & Chloë, 3½oz/100g, each approx 160yd/146m (superwash wool/ organic cotton); worsted weight

- 1 hank in #7519 Waterslide (CC)

HOOKS
- Sizes H/8 and M/13 (5 and 9mm) crochet hooks *or size to obtain gauge*

NOTIONS
- One 15" x 15"/38cm x 38cm pillow form

- Four 1"/25.5mm plastic bone rings

- Removable stitch marker or small safety pin

- Straight pins

- Tracing paper

GAUGE
7 sts and 8 rows = 4"/10cm over sc using larger hook.

Design your
own lettering and
make a matching
set of two or
three pillows!

"Home Cozy Home" Pillow Case

"Home Cozy Home" Pillow Case

3) Pin the tracing paper pieces on the pillow front, evenly spaced from the edges.

4) Following the instructions for chain stitch embroidery on page 20, embroider the design using CC. Secure with a knot and weave in the ends.

ASSEMBLY

1) Place front on work surface, so wrong side is facing up and bottom edge is at bottom.

2) Place lower back on top, so right side is facing up and bottom edge is at bottom.

3) Place upper back on top, so right side is facing and top edge is at top. Upper back will overlap lower back.

4) Pin pieces together around all four sides. Turn assembled piece so front of pillow is facing.

5) To join edges together with sc, work as follows: with smaller hook and CC, make a slip knot and place on the hook.

6) With front facing, insert hook into first sc at right-hand edge of front and first sc at right-hand edge of upper back, then sc pieces together. Continue to sc through matching sts on front and back to last pair of stitches, work 2 sc in last pair of stitches for corner.

7) Turn to side edge, sc evenly to bottom edge, working through all three layers where upper and lower back overlap.

8) Turn to bottom edge, work 2 sc in first pair of stitches for corner, sc to

last pair of stitches, work 2 sc in last pair of stitches for corner.

9) Turn to side edge, sc evenly to top edge, working through all three layers where upper and lower back overlap. Sc in same stitch as beginning sc, then join rnd with a sl st in first sc.

Fasten off. Weave in the ends, and snip the excess.

10) Sew on buttons to lower back, matching buttonholes on upper back flap.

11) Insert pillow form into pillow, then fasten buttons into buttonholes. ◼

Crochet Edge Frames

Display your favorite memories inside these cute crochet frames. Add a colorful edging to a sturdy photo frame, place a photo or art print inside, and hang it on the wall. You can show off a special memory and your crochet skills all at once!

FINISHED DIMENSIONS
PICOT RUFFLE FRAME
7" x 8¾"/18cm x 22cm
SHELL STITCH FRAME
6¾" x 9"/17cm x 23cm
PEARL SHELL FRAME
13" x 16"/33cm x 40.5cm

STITCH GLOSSARY
Picot Ch 3, 1 sc in 2nd ch from hook.

PICOT RUFFLE FRAME
This edging can be used on any size frame. Make sure you are working the edge pattern over a multiple of 3 sts.

PREPARE PHOTO MAT
1) Place a 5" x 7"/12.5cm x 17.5cm photo mat front side down on the work surface.
2) Across one short edge, measure and mark for first corner hole, ¼"/5mm from the right-hand edge and ¼"/5mm from the top edge.
3) For the second corner hole, measure and mark ¼"/5mm from the left-hand edge and ¼"/5mm from the same top edge.
4) For the third and fourth corner holes, turn mat so opposite short edge is at top. Repeat steps 2 and 3.

Apply four photo corners to each of the small photo frames.

5) Measure and mark for 4 more holes evenly spaced between corner holes along each short edge.
5) Measure and mark for 7 more holes evenly spaced between corner holes along each long edge.
6) Punch out holes.

YARN
I Love This Cotton! by Hobby Lobby, 3oz/85g, each approx 153yd/140m (cotton); worsted weight

• 1 ball each in #258 Pistache Sparkle (A) and #42 Orangeade (B)

Cotton DK by Debbie Bliss, 1¾oz/50g, each approx 92yd/84m (pure cotton); DK weight

• 1 ball in #13058 Indian Pink (C)

HOOK
• Size E/4 (3.5mm) crochet hook

NOTIONS
• Two 5" x 7"/12.5cm x 17.5cm pre-cut photo mats in white (suitable for 4" x 6"/10cm x 15cm photos)

• One 11" x 14"/28cm x 35.5cm pre-cut photo mat in white (suitable for 8" x 10"/20.5cm x 25.5cm photo)

• Hole punch

• Photo corners (for small frames) and repositional adhesive (for large frame)

• Pencil

GAUGE
Gauge is not important for this project.

Crochet Edge Frames

CROCHET EDGING

Using A, make a slip knot and place on the hook. With front side of mat facing, insert hook into any corner hole, then join yarn with a sl st in hole.

Rnd 1 (RS) Ch 3, *sl st in next hole, ch 3; rep from * to next corner hole, work (sl st, ch 3, sl st) in corner hole; rep from * around to first corner hole, work (sl st, ch 3) in corner hole, join rnd with a sl st in top of beg ch-3.

Rnd 2 Ch 1, work 3 sc in each ch-3 sp around, join rnd with a sl st in ch-1.

Rnd 3 Ch 1, sc in each sc around, join with a sl st in ch-1.

Rnd 4 Sl st in back loop of first sc, *make a Picot, ch 1, skip 2 sc, sl st in back loop of next sc; rep from * around, join rnd with a sl st in first sl st. Fasten off. Weave in ends and snip the excess.

SHELL STITCH FRAME

This pattern can be used on any size frame as long as you have a multiple of 6 sts.

PREPARE PHOTO MAT

Repeat steps 1–4 same as picot ruffle frame.

5) Measure and mark for 6 more holes evenly spaced between corner holes along each short edge.

5) Measure and mark for 8 more holes evenly spaced between corner holes along each long edge.

6) Punch out holes.

CROCHET EDGING

Using B, make a slip knot and place on the hook. With front side of mat facing, insert hook into any corner hole, then join yarn with a sl st in hole.

Rnd 1 (RS) Ch 2, *sl st in next hole, ch 2; rep from * to next corner hole, work (sl st, ch 3, sl st) in corner hole, ch 2; rep from * around to first corner hole, work (sl st ch 3) in corner hole, join rnd with a sl st in top of beg sl st.

Rnd 2 Ch 1, work 2 sc in each ch-2 sp and 3 sc in each corner ch-3 sp around, join rnd with a sl st in ch-1.

Rnd 3 Ch 1, sc in first sc, *skip 2 sc, work 5 dc in next sc, skip 2 sc, sc in next sc; rep from * around, join rnd with a sl st in first sc. Fasten off. Weave in ends and snip the excess.

PEARL SHELL FRAME

This edge pattern can be used on any size frame mat, as long as you have a multiple of 6 sts.

PREPARE PHOTO MAT

1) Place the 11" x 14"/28cm x 35.5cm photo mat, front side down, on the work surface. Repeat steps 2–4 same as picot ruffle frame.

5) Measure and mark for 10 more holes evenly spaced between corner holes along each short edge.

6) Measure and mark for 16 more holes evenly spaced between corner holes along each long edge.

7) Punch out holes.

CROCHET EDGING

Using C, make a slip knot and place on the hook. With front side of mat facing, insert hook into any corner hole, then join yarn with a sl st in hole.

Rnd 1 (RS) Ch 3, *sl st in next hole, ch 3; rep from * to next corner hole, work (sl st, ch 3, sl st) in corner hole; rep from * around to first corner hole, work (sl st, ch 3) in corner hole, join rnd with a sl st in top of beg ch-3.

Rnd 2 Ch 1, *sc in next sl st, work 3 sc in next ch-3 sp; rep from * around, join rnd with a sl st in first sc.

Rnd 3 Ch 1, sc in same sp as joining, *work 3 sc in next sc, sc in next 5 sc; rep from * around, end last rep sc in last 3 sc, join rnd with a sl st in first sc.

Rnd 4 Ch 3, skip first 2 sc, *work 3 dc in center stitch of next 3-sc group, ch 2, skip 2 sc, sc in next sc, ch 2, skip 2 sc; rep from * around, end work 3 dc in center sc of last 3-sc group, ch 2, skip 2 sc, join rnd with a sl st in last sc. Fasten off. Weave in ends and snip the excess.

ASSEMBLY

1) For small frames, apply a photo corner in each corner for mounting pictures.

2) For large frame, mount picture using repositional adhesive. ■

Yarn Bag Makeover

You only need a few yarn scraps and a plain tote to make your own crochet project bag! Keep all of your yarn and essential tools tucked inside for when you want to take your projects along with you out in the world.

FINISHED DIMENSIONS
POCKET
Width 8"/20.5cm
Height 6¾"/17cm

NOTE
When changing colors, draw new color through last 2 loops on hook to complete last stitch, then turn.

POCKET
With color A, ch 16.
Row 1 Sc in 2nd ch from hook and in each ch across—15 sc. Turn.
Rows 2–11 Ch 1, sc in each sc across. Turn.
Row 12 Ch 1, sc in each sc across, changing to color B. Turn.
Rows 13–17 With color B, sc in each sc across. Turn. Fasten off.

CUSTOMIZE A POCKET TO FIT YOUR TOTE
Measure, then cut out scrap paper to the desired size of your pocket. Using yarn and hook size recommended, make a ch to the width of your paper template. Work in sc, following pocket instructions above, changing colors for the last few rows to create a color block look.

HANDLES
Make a slip knot on your crochet hook. Hold the hook with the yarn underneath the handle. Sc as you would normally, over the handle. Repeat this process until the entire handle is covered. Fasten off and weave in the ends. Repeat for the second handle.

ASSEMBLY
1) Position the pocket in the center of the tote bag and secure it in place with safety pins.
2) Using matching embroidery thread for each color section, sew side and bottom edges in place, leaving top edge open. ∎

YARN
Outer by Spud & Chloë, 3½oz/100g, each approx 60yd/55m (superwash wool/organic cotton); super bulky weight

• 1 hank each in #7211 Rocket (A) and #7214 Ballerina (B)

HOOK
• Size M/13 (9mm) crochet hook *or size to obtain gauge*

NOTIONS
• Plain canvas tote bag

• Six-strand embroidery floss in matching colors

• Sewing needle

• Safety pins

• Scrap paper

• Measuring tape

GAUGE
8 sts and 10 rows = 4"/10cm over sc using size M/13 (9mm) hook.

Experiment with different weights and colors of yarn for a look that suits your style.

Ombré Baskets in Three Sizes

I love experimenting with gradient effects with a variety of yarn colorways. I decided to try this on a trio of baskets. Pile up your yarn inside the large, medium, and small baskets to display in your craft room or anywhere you'd like to keep your prized fibers close by.

FINISHED DIMENSIONS
LARGE
Circumference 37"/94cm
Height 9½"/24cm
MEDIUM
Circumference 32"/81cm
Height 7½"/19cm
SMALL
Circumference 25¼"/64cm
Height 5½"/14cm

NOTE
When changing colors, draw new color through last 2 loops on hook to complete last st.

HOW TO MAKE AN ADJUSTABLE RING
1) To begin, wrap the yarn loosely around 2 fingers, the loose tail near your fingertips and the working yarn to the inside.
2) With the crochet hook, bring the working strand under the outside strand, then draw a loop through.
3) Draw through another loop to complete the single crochet. When all the stitches called for have been worked into the ring, close the ring by pulling the loose tail.

STITCH GLOSSARY
BPsc (Back Post single crochet) Yo, insert hook from back to front around post of dc of the rnd below, yo and draw up a loop, yo and draw through 2 loops on the hook.

YARN
Outer by Spud & Chloë, 3½oz/100g, each approx 60yd/55m (superwash wool/organic cotton); super bulky weight

LARGE
• 2 hanks each in #7214 Ballerina (A), #7206 Sunkissed (B), and #7211 Rocket (C)

MEDIUM
• 2 hanks in #7218 Fearless (A)

• 1 hank each in #7208 Cornsilk (B) and #7219 Buoy (C)

SMALL
• 1 hank each in #7207 Bayou (A), #7213 Bubble (B), and #7216 Snow Day

HOOK
• Size L/11 (8mm) crochet hook *or size to obtain gauge*

GAUGE
8 sts and 5 rnds = 4"/10cm over dc using size L/11 (8mm) hook.

These baskets serve double duty: using up your yarn stash and showing it off!

Ombré Baskets in Three Sizes

LARGE BASKET

BOTTOM

With color A, make an adjustable ring.

Rnd 1 Ch 3 (counts as 1 dc), work 11 dc in the ring, tighten the ring, join rnd with a sl st in top of ch-3—12 dc.

Rnd 2 Ch 3, work 2 dc in each dc around, join rnd with a sl st—24 dc.

Rnd 3 Ch 3, *work 2 dc in the next dc, dc in the next dc; rep from * around, join rnd with a sl st in top of ch-3—36 dc.

Rnd 4 Ch 3, *work 2 dc in the next dc, dc in the next 2 dc; rep from * around, join rnd with a sl st in top of ch-3—48 dc.

Rnd 5 Ch 3, *work 2 dc in the next dc, dc in the next 3 dc; rep from * around, join rnd with a sl st in top of ch-3—60 dc.

Rnd 6 Ch 3, *work 2 dc in the next dc, dc in the next 4 dc; rep from * around, join rnd with a sl st in top of ch-3—72 dc.

SIDES

Next rnd is the set-up rnd to begin working the sides.

Rnd 7 Ch 1, BPsc around each dc around, join rnd with a sl st in ch-1—72 sc.

Rnd 8 Ch 3, dc in each sc around, join rnd with a sl st in top of ch-3.

Rnd 9 Ch 3, dc in each dc around, join rnd with a sl st in top of ch-3.

Rnd 10 Ch 3, dc in dc around, changing to color B when completing the last st, join rnd with a sl st in top of ch-3.

Rnds 11 and 12 Ch 3, dc in each dc around, join rnd with a sl st in top of ch-3.

Rnd 13 Ch 3, dc in each dc around, changing to color C when completing the last st, join rnd with a sl st in top of ch-3.

Rnds 14–16 Ch 3, dc in each dc around, join rnd with a sl st in top of ch-3. Fasten off. Weave in all ends.

MEDIUM BASKET

BOTTOM

With color A, make an adjustable ring. Work rnds 1–5 as for Large Basket—60 dc.

SIDES

Next rnd is the set-up rnd to begin working the sides.

Rnd 6 Ch 1, BPsc around each dc around, join rnd with a sl st in ch-1—60 sc.

Rnd 7 Ch 3, dc in each sc around, join rnd with a sl st in top of ch-3.

Rnd 8 Ch 3, dc in each dc around, join rnd with a sl st in top of ch-3.

Rnd 9 Ch 3, dc in each dc around, changing to color B when completing the last st, join rnd with a sl st in top of ch-3.

Rnds 10 and 11 Ch 3, dc in each dc around, join rnd with a sl st in top of ch-3.

Rnd 12 Ch 3, dc in each dc around, changing to color C when completing the last st, join rnd with a sl st in top of ch-3.

Rnds 13–15 Ch 3, dc in each dc around, join rnd with a sl st in top of ch-3. Fasten off. Weave in all ends.

SMALL BASKET

BOTTOM

With color A, make an adjustable ring. Work rnds 1–4 as for Large Basket—48 dc.

SIDES

Next rnd is the set-up rnd to begin working the sides.

Rnd 5 Ch 1, BPsc around each dc around, join rnd with a sl st in ch-1—48 sc.

Rnd 6 Ch 3, dc in each sc around, join rnd with a sl st in top of ch-3.

Rnd 7 Ch 3, dc in each dc around, changing to color B when completing the last st, join rnd with a sl st in top of ch-3.

Rnd 8 Ch 3, dc in each dc around, join rnd with a sl st in top of ch-3.

Rnd 9 Ch 3, dc in each dc around, changing to color C when completing the last st, join rnd with a sl st in top of ch-3.

Rnds 10–14 Ch 3, dc in each dc around, join rnd with a sl st in top of ch-3. Fasten off. Weave in all ends. ■

Crochet Hook Organizer

Store your hooks, scissors, stitch markers, and other tools inside this handy crochet portfolio. One side of the folder has pockets for up to ten crochet hooks, and the other has a place to store your favorite journal for jotting down pattern notes. Slide two pieces of chipboard in between the front and back sections to make the case sturdy as well as stylish.

FINISHED DIMENSIONS
Width 11¾"/30cm (closed)
Height 13¼"/33.5cm

NOTE
When changing colors, draw new color through last 2 loops on hook to complete last stitch, then turn.

STITCH GLOSSARY
sc2tog [Insert hook in next sc, yo and draw up a loop] twice, yo and draw through all 3 loops on hook.

FRONT COVER
With color A, ch 40.
Row 1 Sc in the 2nd ch from the hook and in each ch across—39 sc. Turn.
Rows 7–14 Ch 1, sc in each sc across. Turn.
Row 15 Ch 1, sc in each sc across, changing to B. Turn.
Row 16 Ch 1, sc in each sc across. Turn.
Row 17 Ch 1, sc in each sc across, changing to A. Turn.
Row 18 Ch 1, sc in each sc across. Turn.
Row 19 Ch 1, sc in each sc across, changing to B. Turn.

Row 20 Ch 1, sc in each sc across. Turn.
Row 21 Ch 1, sc in each sc across, changing to A. Turn.
Row 22 Ch 1, sc in each sc across, changing to B. Turn.
Row 23 Ch 1, sc in each sc across. Turn.
Row 24 Ch 1, sc in each sc across, changing to A. Turn.
Row 25 Ch 1, sc in each sc across, changing to B. Turn.
Rows 26–30 Ch 1, sc in each sc across. Turn.
Row 31 Ch 1, sc in each sc across, changing to A. Turn.
Row 32 Ch 1, sc in each sc across, changing to B. Turn.
Row 33 Ch 1, sc in each sc across. Turn.
Row 34 Ch 1, sc in each sc across, changing to A. Turn.
Row 35 Ch 1, sc in each sc across, changing to B. Turn.
Row 36 Ch 1, sc in each sc across. Turn.
Row 37 Ch 1, sc in each sc across, changing to A. Turn.
Row 38 Ch 1, sc in each sc across. Turn.
Row 39 Ch 1, sc in each sc across, changing to B. Turn.

YARN
Sweater by Spud & Chloë, 3½oz/100g, each approx 160yd/146m (superwash wool/ organic cotton); worsted weight

- 4 hanks in #7527 Billiard (A)

- 1 hank each in #7513 Jelly Bean (B), #7528 Life Jacket (C), #7510 Splash (D), #7500 Ice Cream (E), #7522 Penguin (F), and #7521 Beluga (G)

HOOK
- Size H/8 (5mm) crochet hook *or size to obtain gauge*

NOTIONS
- Two 11½" x 13"/ 29cm x 33cm pieces of chipboard

- Three 1"/25.5mm plastic bone rings

- Removable stitch marker or small safety pin

- Straight pins

GAUGE
13 sts and 18 rows = 4"/10cm over sc using size H/8 (5mm) hook.

Keep the organizer on your craft desk or nearby on the couch while you work on a project!

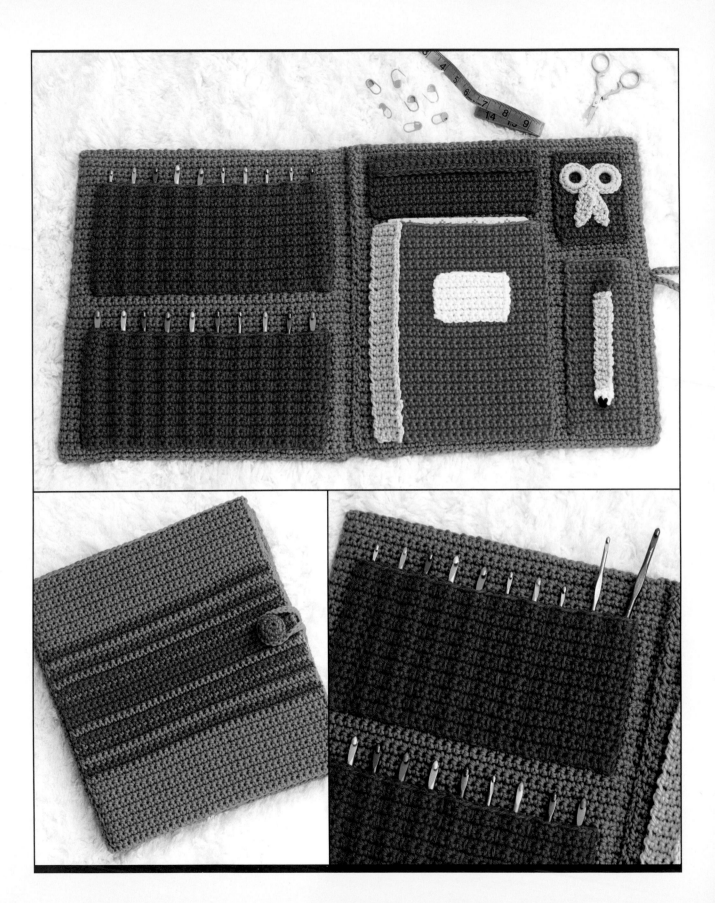

Crochet Hook Organizer

Row 40 Ch 1, sc in each sc across. Turn.
Row 41 Ch 1, sc in each sc across, changing to A. Turn.
Rows 42–56 Ch 1, sc in each sc across. Turn. Fasten off, leaving a long tail for sewing.

BACK COVER

With color A, ch 40.
Row 1 Sc in the 2nd ch from the hook and in each ch across—39 sc. Turn.
Rows 2–56 Ch 1, sc in each sc across. Turn. Fasten off, leaving a long tail for sewing.

FRONT INSIDE COVER

With color A, ch 42.
Row 1 Sc in the 2nd ch from the hook and in each ch across—41 sc. Turn.
Rows 2–56 Ch 1, sc in each sc across. Turn. Fasten off, leaving a long tail for sewing.

BACK INSIDE COVER

Work as for front inside cover.

CROCHET HOOK POCKETS (MAKE 2)

With color B, ch 35.
Row 1 Sc in the 2nd ch from the hook and in each ch across—34 sc. Turn.
Rows 2–20 Ch 1, sc in each sc across. Turn. Fasten off, leaving a long tail for sewing.

NOTEBOOK POCKET

With color C, ch 22.
Row 1 Sc in the 2nd ch from the hook and in each ch across—21 sc. Turn.
Rows 2–38 Ch 1, sc in each sc across. Turn. Fasten off, leaving a long tail for sewing.

SPINE
With color D, ch 5.
Row 1 Sc in the 2nd ch from the hook and in each ch across—4 sc. Turn.
Rows 2–38 Ch 1, sc in each sc across. Turn. Fasten off, leaving a long tail for sewing.

LABEL
With color E, ch 11.
Row 1 Sc in the 2nd ch from the hook and in each ch across—10 sc. Turn.
Rows 2–8 Ch 1, sc in each sc across. Turn. Fasten off, leaving a long tail for sewing.

ASSEMBLE THE NOTEBOOK POCKET
1) Position the spine slightly over the left side edge of the notebook pocket. Sew in place. Weave in the ends.
2) Position the label on the pocket, 2¼"/5.5cm from top edge and 1½"/4cm from right side edge. Sew in place. Weave in the ends.

PENCIL POCKET

With color C, ch 11.

Row 1 Sc in the 2nd ch from the hook and in each ch across—10 sc. Turn.
Rows 2–30 Ch 1, sc in each sc across. Turn. Fasten off, leaving a long tail for sewing.

PENCIL
With color B, ch 3.
Eraser
Row 1 Sc in the 2nd ch from the hook and in each ch across—2 sc. Turn.
Row 2 Ch 1, sc in each sc across, changing to G. Turn.
Ferrule
Row 3 Ch 1, sc in each sc across. Turn.
Row 4 Ch 1, sc in each sc across, changing to D. Turn.
Shaft
Rows 5–19 Ch 1, sc in each sc across. Turn.
Row 20 Ch 1, sc in each sc across, changing to E. Turn.
Point
Rows 21 and 22 Ch 1, sc in each sc across. Turn.
Row 23 Ch 1, sc2tog—1 sc. Fasten off, leaving a long tail for sewing.

ASSEMBLE THE PENCIL POCKET
1) For the pencil tip, cut a length of color F and knot the end.
2) Thread the yarn through a tapestry needle and bring the yarn up through the bottom of the pencil point

Crochet Hook Organizer

from back to front. Bring the needle up and down through the pencil point to create a "V" shape. Weave in the ends.

3) Position the pencil on the pocket so it is centered from side to side and top to bottom. Sew in place. Weave in the ends.

SCISSOR POCKET

With color B, ch 11.

Row 1 Sc in the 2nd ch from the hook and in each ch across—10 sc. Turn.

Rows 2–17 Ch 1, sc in each sc across. Turn. Fasten off, leaving a long tail for sewing.

SCISSOR BLADES (MAKE 2)

With color G, ch 2.

Row 1 Sc in the 2nd ch from the hook and in each ch across—1 sc. Turn.

Row 2 Ch 1, work 2 sc in sc across—2 sc. Turn.

Rows 3–7 Ch 1, sc in each sc across. Turn. Fasten off, leaving a long tail for sewing.

SCISSOR EYE (MAKE 2)

With color D, make a slip knot and place on hook.

Rnd 1 (RS) Working fairly tightly, sc over plastic bone ring until ring is completely covered, join rnd with a sl st in first sc. Fasten off, leaving a long tail for sewing.

ASSEMBLE THE SCISSOR POCKET

1) Sew the bottom edge of each blade to the edge of an eye.

2) Overlap one blade on top of the other blade, criss-crossing them as shown.

3) Sew the overlapping section together to secure.

4) For the screw, use color D to embroider a French knot, following the steps on page 22. Secure with a knot on the wrong side and weave in the ends.

5) Position the scissors on the pocket centered from side to side and top to bottom. Sew in place. Weave in the ends.

NOTIONS POCKET

POCKET

With color B, ch 25.

Row 1 Sc in the 2nd ch from the hook and in each ch across—24 sc. Turn.

Rows 2–10 Ch 1, sc in each sc across. Turn. Fasten off, leaving a long tail for sewing.

FLAP

With color B, ch 25.

Row 1 Sc in the 2nd ch from the hook and in each ch across—24 sc. Turn.

Rows 2–4 Ch 1, sc in each sc across. Turn. Fasten off, leaving a long tail for sewing.

BUTTON

With color C, ch 2.

Rnd 1 Work 6 sc in the 2nd ch from the hook. Do not join. Mark the last stitch made with the stitch marker or safety pin. You will be working in a spiral, marking the last stitch made with the stitch marker or safety pin to indicate end of rnd.

Rnd 2 Work 2 sc in each sc around—12 sc.

Rnd 3 Sc in each sc around.

Rnd 4 [Sc2tog] 6 times, inserting a bone ring before closing opening, join rnd with a sl st in first sc. Fasten off, leaving a long tail for sewing.

BUTTON LOOP

With color A, ch 32. Turn ch so bottom loops are at top.

Row 1 Sc in the 2nd bottom loop from the hook and in each bottom loop across, join with a sl st in the first sc, forming a loop. Fasten off, leaving a long tail for sewing.

ASSEMBLY

1) For front inside cover, pin the first crochet hook pocket ½"/1.5cm from bottom edge and centered side to side. Pin second crochet hook pocket 1¾"/4.5cm above the first and centered side to side. Sew each in place, leaving the top edge open. Weave in the ends.

2) For each pocket, create ten separate crochet hook compartments. Measure and mark with a pin, at 1"/2.5cm intervals along top and bottom edges.

3) For each compartment, cut a long length of color B. Sew backstitches in a straight line between each corresponding pin mark.

4) For the back inside cover, pin the notebook pocket ½"/1.5cm from left side edge and ½"/1.5cm from bottom edge. Sew in place, leaving the top edge open. Weave in the ends.

5) Pin the pencil pocket ½"/1.5cm from right side edge of the notebook pocket and ½"/1.5cm from bottom edge. Sew in place, leaving the top edge open. Weave in the ends.

6) Center the scissors pocket above the pencil pocket, so top edge of scissors pocket is ¾"/2cm from top edge of back inside cover. Sew in place, leaving the top edge open. Weave in the ends.

7) For the notions pocket, first center the pocket section above the notebook pocket, so bottom edge of pocket is ⅜"/1cm from top edge of notebook. Position the flap across the top edge of the pocket section. Lap the bottom edge of the flap over the top 2 rows of the pocket section. Pin pieces in place. Sew in place around all sides (top edge of flap, each side flap/pocket and bottom edge of pocket); inside top edge of pocket will be open. Weave in the ends.

8) Place front cover right side up on work surface so bottom edge is at bottom. Position the button 1"/2.5cm

from right-hand edge and centered in wide center stripe. Sew in place. Weave in the ends.

9) Place front cover, right side up, on front inside cover, so bottom, top, and right-hand edges are even. Front inside cover is 2 stitches wider than the front cover. Sew pieces together, leaving left-hand edges open. Insert chipboard. Sew left-hand edge of front cover to front inside cover, leaving the 2-stitch-wide flange free. Weave in the ends.

10) Fold button loop in half and tack edges together. Weave in the ends. Set aside.

11) Place back cover, right side up, on back inside cover, so bottom, top, and left-hand edges are even. Back inside cover is 2 stitches wider than the back cover.

12) On center of left-hand edge of the covers, insert ends of button loop between the layers; pin in place. Sew pieces together, leaving right-hand edges open. Insert chipboard. Sew right-hand edge of back cover to back inside cover, leaving the 2-stitch-wide flange free. Weave in the ends.

13) Sew the inside front cover flanges together. Weave in the ends. ■

Heart Pocket Apron

This apron was inspired by a Saturday-morning marathon of *I Love Lucy* reruns. Lucy was up to her usual antics while sporting an adorable apron with a single heart pocket. I decided to try my hand at a shell stitch crochet version and infuse it with a little Lucy flair!

FINISHED DIMENSIONS

APRON
Width 21½"/54.5cm (excluding sash ties)
Length 21"/53.5cm (including sash)
HEART POCKET
Width 5¾"/14.5cm
Height 5¼"/13.5cm

NOTES

1) When changing colors, draw new color through last 2 loops on hook to complete last st, then turn.

2) To join yarn with a sc, make a slip knot 5"/12.5cm from end of yarn and place on hook. Insert hook into stitch, yo and draw up a loop, yo and draw through both loops on hook.

STITCH GLOSSARY

Shell st Work (2 dc, ch 1, 2 dc) in same ch-1 sp.

sc2tog [Insert hook in next sc, yo and draw up a loop] twice, yo and draw through all 3 loops on hook.

APRON

With color A, ch 78.
Row 1 (RS) Sc in the 2nd ch from the hook, *skip next 3 ch, Shell stitch in next ch; rep from * to the last 4 ch, end skip next 3 ch, sc in last ch—18 shell sts. Turn.

Row 2 Ch 3 (counts as 1 dc), dc in first sc, *Shell stitch in next ch-1 sp; rep from *, end work 2 dc in last sc. Turn.

Row 3 Ch 1, sc in first dc, *Shell stitch in next ch-1 sp; rep from *, end sc in top of ch-3 of row below. Turn.

Rows 4–21 Rep rows 2 and 3 nine times more.

Row 22 Rep row 2, changing to color B.

Row 23 With color B, rep row 3, changing to color A.

Row 24 With color A, rep row 2, changing to color B.

Row 25 With color B, rep row 3.

Row 26 With color B, rep row 2, changing to color A.

Row 27 With color A, rep row 3, changing to color B.

Rows 28–32 With color B, rep rows 2 and 3 twice more, then row 2 once. Fasten off and weave in ends.

HEART POCKET (MAKE 2)

With color C, ch 4.
Row 1 (RS) Sc in the 2nd ch from the hook and in each ch across—3 sc. Turn.

YARN

Sweater by Spud & Chloe, 3½oz/100g, each approx 160yd/146m (superwash wool/ organic cotton); worsted weight

• 3 hanks in #7521 Beluga (A)

• 2 hanks in #7519 Waterslide (B)

• 1 hank in #7518 Barn (C)

HOOK

• Size H/8 (5mm) crochet hook *or size to obtain gauge*

NOTIONS

• Straight pins

GAUGE

14 sts and 7 rows = 4"/10cm over shell stitch pat using size H/8 (5mm) hook.

This beautiful texture is accentuated by pops of color in the details.

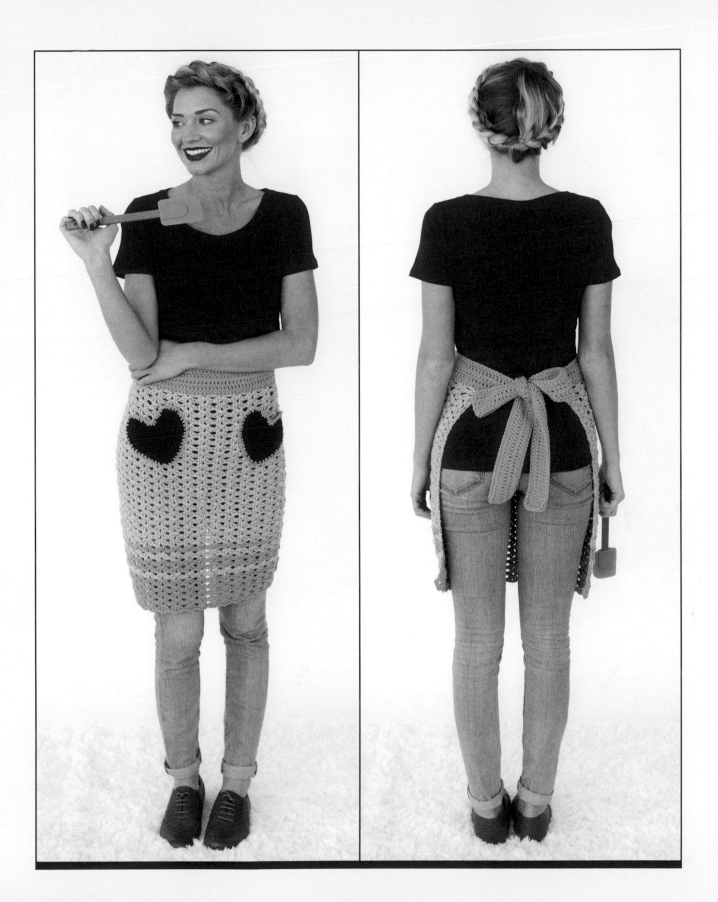

Heart Pocket Apron

Row 2 Ch 1, work 2 sc in the first sc, sc in the next sc, work 2 sc in the last sc—5 sc. Turn.

Row 3 Ch 1, work 2 sc in the first sc, sc in the next 3 sc, work 2 sc in the last sc—7 sc. Turn.

Row 4 Ch 1, work 2 sc in the first sc, sc in the next 5 sc, work 2 sc in the last sc—9 sc. Turn.

Row 5 Ch 1, work 2 sc in the first sc, sc in the next 7 sc, work 2 sc in the last sc—11 sc. Turn.

Row 6 Ch 1, work 2 sc in the first sc, sc in the next 9 sc, work 2 sc in the last sc—13 sc. Turn.

Row 7 Ch 1, sc in each sc across. Turn.

Row 8 Ch 1, work 2 sc in the first sc, sc in the next 11 sc, work 2 sc in the last sc—15 sc. Turn.

Row 9 Ch 1, sc in each sc across. Turn.

Row 10 Ch 1, work 2 sc in the first sc, sc in the next 13 sc, work 2 sc in the last sc—17 sc. Turn.

Rows 11–14 Ch 1, sc in each sc across. Turn.

UPPER RIGHT SECTION

Row 15 Ch 1, sc in first 8 sc, leaving rem 9 sts unworked. Turn.

Row 16 Ch 1, sc2tog, sc in each sc across—7 sc. Turn.

Row 17 Ch 1, sc2tog, sc in the next 3 sc, sc2tog—5 sc. Turn.

Row 18 Ch 1, sc2tog, sc in the next sc, sc2tog—3 sc. Turn.

Row 19 Ch 1, sc2tog, sc in the last sc—2 sc. Fasten off and weave in the end.

UPPER LEFT SECTION

Row 15 Skip the center sc, join color C with an sc in the next sc, then sc in last 7 sc—8 sc. Turn.

Row 16 Ch 1, sc in the next 6 sc, sc2tog—7 sc. Turn.

Row 17 Ch 1, sc2tog, sc in the next 3 sc, sc2tog—5 sc. Turn.

Row 18 Ch 1, sc2tog, sc in the next sc, sc2tog—3 sc. Turn.

Row 19 Ch 1, sc in the first sc, sc2tog—2 sc. Fasten off and weave in the end.

EDGING

With the right side facing, join color B with an sc in the center sc between the two upper sections.

Rnd 1 Making sure that the work lies flat, sc evenly around the entire outer edge, working 3 sc in the bottom tip, join with a sl st in first sc. Fasten off and weave in the end.

SASH

With color B, ch 246.

Row 1 Dc in the 4th ch from the hook and in each ch across—243 dc. Turn.

Rows 2 and 3 Ch 3, dc in each dc across. Turn.

EDGING

Rnd 1 Ch 2, hdc in each dc and row around entire outer edge, join rnd with a sl st in top of beginning ch-2. Fasten off and weave in the end.

ASSEMBLY

1) Pin the heart pockets at a slight angle to the upper middle section of the apron. Place the hearts at an equal distance from the edges and from the middle.

2) Using color B, sew the outer edging of the pockets to the apron, leaving the top sections of the hearts open. Weave in the ends.

3) Pin the sash in place along the top edge of the apron, leaving 25"/63.5cm-long ties extending from each side edge.

4) Cut a long length of color B and sew the sash to the apron. Weave in the ends. ■

Teacup Coasters

Always looking for a place to rest your teacup? To the rescue: a coaster! I come from a long line of proud tea lovers, including my grandfather, my grandmother, and my mom. We love to sip "a spot of tea" on chilly afternoons, and this adorable coaster makes the experience even more enjoyable!

FINISHED DIMENSIONS
Width 4¾"/12cm
Height 4"/10cm

NOTE
When changing colors, draw new color through last 2 loops on hook to complete last st, then turn.

STITCH GLOSSARY
sc2tog [Insert hook in next sc, yo and draw up a loop] twice, yo and draw through all 3 loops on hook.

COLORWAYS
Version I Grass (A), Splash (B), and Ice Cream (C).
Version II Waterslide (A), Splash (B), and Ice Cream (C).
Version III Splash (A), Lilac (B), and Ice Cream (C).
Version IV Lilac (A), Grass (B), and Ice Cream (C).

TEACUP BACK
With color A, ch 7.
Row 1 Sc in the 2nd ch from the hook and in each ch across—6 sc. Turn.
Row 2 Ch 1, work 2 sc in the first sc, sc in the next 4 sc, work 2 sc in the last sc—8 sc. Turn.
Row 3 Ch 1, work 2 sc in the first sc, sc in the next 6 sc, work 2 sc in the last sc—10 sc. Turn.
Row 4 Ch 1, work 2 sc in the first sc, sc in the next 8 sc, work 2 sc in the last sc—12 sc. Turn.
Row 5 Ch 1, work 2 sc in the first sc, sc in the next 10 sc, work 2 sc in the last sc—14 sc. Turn.
Row 6 Ch 1, work 2 sc in the first sc, sc in the next 12 sc, work 2 sc in the last sc—16 sc. Turn.
Rows 7 and 8 Ch 1, sc in each sc across—16 sc. Turn.
Row 9 Ch 1, sc in the first 8 sc, work 2 sc in the next sc, sc in the last 7 sc—17 sc. Turn.
Rows 10–17 Ch 1, sc in each sc across. Turn. Fasten off, leaving a long tail for sewing.

YARN
Sweater by Spud & Chloë, 3½oz/100g, each approx 160yd/146m (superwash wool/ organic cotton); worsted weight

• 1 hank each in #7502 Grass, #7519 Waterslide, #7510 Splash, #7523 Lilac, and #7500 Ice Cream

HOOK
• Size H/8 (5mm) crochet hook *or size to obtain gauge*

GAUGE
13 sts and 18 rows = 4"/10cm over sc using size H/8 (5mm) hook.

Pair this coaster with the placemat on page 79 for a crochet place setting!

Teacup Coasters

TEACUP FRONT

With color A, work as for back to row 8—16 sc.

Row 9 Ch 1, sc in the first 8 sc, work 2 sc in the next sc, sc in the last 7 sc, changing to color B—17 sc. Turn.

Row 10 (RS) With color B, ch 1, sc in each sc across. Turn.

Row 11 Ch 1, sc in the first sc, *ch 3, skip the next 3 sc, sc in the next sc; rep from * across. Turn.

Row 12 Ch 1, sc in the first sc, *work 3 sc in the next ch-3 sp, sc in the next sc; rep from *, changing to color A. Turn.

Rows 13–16 With color A, ch 1, sc in each sc across. Turn. Fasten off, leaving a long tail for sewing.

HANDLE

With color A, ch 12. Turn ch so bottom loops are at top.

Row 1 Sc in the 2nd bottom loop from the hook and in each bottom loop across—11 sc. Fasten off, leaving a long tail for sewing.

TEA BAG

With color C, ch 5.

Row 1 Sc in the 2nd ch from the hook and in each ch across—4 sc. Turn.

Rows 2 and 3 Ch 1, sc in each sc across. Turn.

Row 4 Ch 1, [sc2tog] twice—2 sc. Turn.

Row 5 Sc2tog—1 sc. Fasten off, leaving a long tail for sewing and for tea bag "string."

ASSEMBLY

1) Weave in all the ends on the teacup pieces except for the long tails needed for assembly.

2) Line up the front and back pieces with right sides facing out.

3) Sew the pieces together.

4) Sew the handle to the right-hand edge of the teacup.

5) Attach the tea bag to the upper left front of the teacup, leaving a 1"/2.5cm tea bag "string," as shown.

6) Weave in remaining ends and snip the excess. ■

"Enjoy" Place Setting Placemat

Setting the table was never so much fun! Stitch together a set of these adorable crochet placemats to enjoy during home-cooked meals with friends and family.

YARN
Sweater by Spud & Chloë, 3½oz/100g hanks, each approx 160yd/146m (superwash wool/organic cotton); worsted weight

• 2 hanks in #7521 Beluga (A)

• 1 hank each in #7502 Grass (B), #7510 Splash (C), and #7522 Penguin (D)

HOOK
• Size H/8 (5mm) crochet hook *or size to obtain gauge*

NOTIONS
• Straight pins

• Tracing paper

GAUGE
14 sts and 15 rows = 4"/10cm over sc using size H/8 (5mm) hook.

Mix and match the colors of the fork, knife, and plate for a look that suits your personality.

FINISHED DIMENSIONS
PLACEMAT
Width 17"/43cm
Height 14"/35.5cm
PLATE
Diameter 9"/23cm
FORK
Width 1¼"/3cm
Length 7¼"/18.5cm
KNIFE
Width 1"/2.5cm
Length 8¾"/22cm

NOTE
When changing colors, draw new color through last 2 loops on hook to complete last stitch.

MAKING AN ADJUSTABLE RING
1) To begin, wrap the yarn loosely around 2 fingers, the loose tail near your fingertips and the working yarn to the inside.
2) With the crochet hook, bring the working strand under the outside strand, then draw a loop through.

"Enjoy" Place Setting Placemat

3) Draw through another loop to complete the single crochet. When all the stitches called for have been worked into the ring, close the ring by pulling the loose tail.

PLACEMAT

With color A, ch 12.

Rnd 1 Work
2 dc in 4th ch from hook (3 skipped ch count as 1 dc), ch 1, skip next 3 ch, work 3 dc in next ch, ch 1, skip next 3 ch, work ([3 dc, ch 2] twice, 3 dc) in last ch, ch 1, turn ch so bottom loops are at top, skip next 3 loops, work 3 dc in next loop (same loop as 3-dc on top of ch), ch 1, skip next 3 loops, work [3 dc, ch 2] twice in last loop (same loop as beg 2 dc), join rnd with a sl st in beg ch-3.

Rnd 2 Ch 3 (always counts as 1 dc), work 2 dc in last corner ch-2 sp of rnd below, ch 1, *work 3 dc in next ch-1 sp, ch 1*; rep from * once more, [work (3 dc, ch 2, 3 dc) in next corner ch-2 sp, ch 1] twice, rep from * to * twice, end work (3 dc, ch 2, 3 dc) in next corner ch-2 sp, ch 1, work (3 dc, ch 2) in last corner ch-2 sp, join rnd with a sl st in top of beg ch-3.

Rnd 3 Ch 3, work 2 dc in last corner ch-2 sp of rnd below, ch 1, *work 3 dc in next ch-1 sp, ch 1*; rep from * twice more, work (3 dc, ch 2, 3 dc) in next corner ch-2 sp, ch 1, work 3 dc in next ch-1 sp, ch 1, work (3 dc, ch 2, 3 dc) in next corner ch-2 sp, ch 1*, rep from * to * 3 times, end work (3 dc, ch 2, 3 dc) in next corner ch-2 sp, ch 1, work 3 dc in next ch-1 sp, ch 1, work (3 dc, ch 2) in last corner ch-2 sp, join rnd with a sl st in top of beg ch-3.

Rnds 4–12 Ch 3, work 2 dc in last corner ch-2 sp of rnd below, ch 1, ** *work 3 dc in next ch-1 sp, ch 1*; rep from * to next corner ch-2 sp, work (3 dc, ch 2, 3 dc) in corner ch-2 sp, ch 1**, rep from ** to ** twice more, end rep from * to * to last corner ch-2 sp, work (3 dc, ch 2) in last corner ch-2 sp, join rnd with a sl st

"Enjoy" Place Setting Placemat

in top of beg ch-3.

Note At the end of rnd 12, join rnd, changing to color B.

Rnd 13 With B, ch 1, sc in each dc and ch around, join rnd with a sl st in first sc.

Rnd 14 Ch 2, hdc in same sp as joining, ch 1,** *skip next sc, hdc in next sc, ch 1*; rep from * to 1 sc before center sc in next corner, (hdc in next sc, ch 1) 3 times**, rep from ** to ** twice more, end rep from * to * to 1 sc before center sc in last corner, (hdc in next sc, ch 1) twice, join rnd with a sl st in top of beg ch-2. Fasten off. Weave in ends.

PLATE

With color B, make an adjustable ring.

Rnd 1 Ch 3 (counts as 1 dc), work 11 dc in the ring, tighten the ring, join rnd with a sl st in top of ch-3—12 dc.

Rnd 2 Ch 3, work 2 dc in each dc around, join rnd with a sl st—24 dc.

Rnd 3 Ch 3, *work 2 dc in the next dc, dc in the next dc; rep from * around, join rnd with a sl st in top of ch-3—36 dc.

Rnd 4 Ch 3, *work 2 dc in the next dc, dc in the next 2 dc; rep from * around, join rnd with a sl st in top of ch-3—48 dc.

Rnd 5 Ch 3, *work 2 dc in the next dc, dc in the next 3 dc; rep from * around, join rnd with a sl st in top of ch-3—60 dc.

Rnd 6 Ch 3, *work 2 dc in the next dc, dc in the next 4 dc; rep from * around, join rnd with a sl st in top of ch-3, changing to color B—72 dc.

Rnd 7 With B, ch 3, *work 2 dc in the next dc, dc in the next 5 dc; rep from * around, join rnd with a sl st in top of ch-3—84 dc.

Rnd 8 Ch 3, *work 2 dc in the next dc, dc in the next 6 dc; rep from * around, join rnd with a sl st in top of ch-3—96 dc. Fasten off, leaving a long tail for sewing.

FORK
BASE OF TINES
With color C, ch 3.

Row 1 Sc in the 2nd ch from the hook and in each ch across—2 sc. Turn.

Row 2 Ch 1, [work 2 sc in next sc] twice—4 sc. Turn.

Rows 3 and 4 Ch 1, sc in each sc across. Turn.

Row 5 (RS)

First tine

Ch 7, sl st in the 2nd ch from the hook and in next 5 ch, join with a sl st in the first sc of row 4.

Second tine

Ch 7, sl st in the 2nd ch from the hook and in next 5 ch, join with a sl st in the 2nd sc of row 4.

Third tine

Ch 7, sl st in the 2nd ch from the hook and in next 5 ch, join with a sl st in the 3rd sc of row 4.

Fourth tine

Ch 7, sl st in the 2nd ch from the hook and in next 5 ch, join with a sl st in the 4th sc of row 4. Fasten off, leaving a long tail for sewing.

HANDLE
With color C, ch 19. With color A, ch 12. Turn ch so bottom loops are at top.

Rnd 1 (RS)

First side

Sl st in the 2nd bottom loop from the hook, sl st in next 11 loops, sc in next 3 loops, hdc in next loop, dc in next loop, work 5 dc in last loop; turn to top of foundation ch.

Second side

Dc in the first ch, hdc in next ch, sc in next 3 ch, sl st in next 12 ch. Join rnd with a sl st in first sl st. Fasten off, leaving a long tail for sewing.

KNIFE
With color C, ch 32. Turn ch so bottom loops are at top.

Rnd 1 (RS)

First side of blade

Work 3 sc in the 2nd loop from the hook, dc in the next 12 loops, ch 3, join ch with a sl st in same loop as last dc. Continue to work across ch as follows:

First side of handle

Sl st in next 12 loops, sc in next 3 loops, hdc in next loop, dc in next loop, work 5 dc in last loop; turn to top of foundation ch.

Second side of handle and blade

Dc in next ch, hdc in next ch, sc in each rem ch to end, join rnd with a sl st in first sc. Fasten off, leaving a long tail for sewing.

ASSEMBLY
1) Sew base of tines to top of fork handle.

2) Block the pieces to the finished dimensions.

3) Trace the "enjoy" design, on page 80, on the tracing paper.

4) Pin the tracing paper on the plate, evenly spaced from the edges.

5) Following the instructions for chain stitch embroidery on page 20, embroider the design using D. Secure with a knot and weave in the ends.

6) Sew the plate to the center of the placemat.

7) Position the fork to the left of the plate so bottom edge of handle is 2½"/6.5cm from bottom edge of placemat and side edge of center of handle is 2¼"/5.5cm from left side edge of placemat.

8) Position the knife to the right of the plate so bottom edge of handle is 2½"/6.5cm from bottom edge of placemat and side edge is 1¾"/4.5cm from right side edge of placemat. ■

Cottage Tea Cozy

I have always dreamed about moving to the countryside and living in a cottage stuffed with books and yarn—like the one I dreamed up for this teapot cozy. The scalloped roof shingles are created using the beautiful crocodile stitch.

FINISHED DIMENSIONS
Width 11"/28cm
Height 8½"/21.5cm

NOTE
When changing colors, draw new color through last 2 loops on hook to complete last stitch, then turn.

STITCH GLOSSARY
sc2tog [Insert hook in next sc, yo and draw up a loop] twice, yo and draw through all 3 loops on hook.

NOTES ON CROCODILE STITCH
This is a fun stitch to crochet. It's created in an unconventional manner, where all the rows are worked from the right side. Odd rows are made in the conventional way, working horizontally from right to left. Here a framework for the "crocodile scales" is made of a series of 2-dc groups, separated by ch-2's. The even rows are where the scales are worked following a zigzag path back to the beginning of the framework row. Each scale is made by working 5 dc over the first dc of a group, then 5 dc over the second dc of the same group. To do this, you will turn the work so that the bottom loops of the foundation chain are at your left in order to work the first 5 dc.

You will then turn the work so that the bottom loops are at your right to work the second 5 dc.

ROOF (MAKE 2)
With color A, ch 34.
Row 1 (RS) Dc in the 4th ch from the hook (3 skipped ch counts as 1 dc), *ch 2, skip next 2 ch, work 2 dc in next ch; rep from * across—eleven 2-dc groups. Do not turn.
Row 2 (RS) Ch 2, *turn work so bottom loops of beg ch are at left, work 5 dc over first dc, ch 1, turn work so bottom loops are at right, work 5 dc over next dc (one crocodile scale made), skip next 2-dc group; rep from *, end one crocodile scale over last 2-dc group—6 crocodile scales. Do not turn.
Row 3 (RS) Ch 2, *work 2 dc in space in top of next scale, ch 2, working through both thicknesses, work 2 dc in ch-1 between last and next scale and in top of 2-dc group of row below, ch 2; rep from *, end last rep with 2 dc in space in top of last scale, ch 2, join with a sl st in top left corner of scale of row below—eleven 2-dc groups. Do not turn.
Row 4 (RS) Ch 2, skip first 2-dc group, *crocodile scale over next 2-dc group, ch 1, skip next 2-dc group; rep from *, end crocodile scale over next 2-dc

YARN
Blue Faced Leicester Aran by Debbie Bliss, 1¾oz/50g, each approx 82yd/75m (Blue Faced Leicester wool); worsted weight

• 3 balls each in #15 Mint (A) and #14 Duck Egg (B)

• 1 ball each in #08 Red (C), #01 Ecru (D), and #02 Black (E)

HOOK
• Size I/9 (5.5mm) crochet hook *or size to obtain gauge*

NOTION
• Straight pins

GAUGE
12 sts and 18 rows = 4"/10cm over sc using size I/9 (5.5mm) hook.

Now, if only I could shrink down and walk in through the tiny front door!

Cottage Tea Cozy

group, join with a sl st in top right corner of scale below—5 crocodile scales. Do not turn.

Row 5 (RS) Ch 3, dc in same dc of joining, rep from * to * of row 3 eight times, end work 2 dc in space in top of last scale, ch 2, work 2 dc under both ch's of row below—eleven 2-dc groups. Do not turn.

Row 6 (RS) Rep row 2—6 crocodile scales. Do not turn.

Row 7 (RS) Rep row 3—eleven 2-dc groups. Do not turn.

Row 8 (RS) Rep row 4—5 crocodile scales. Do not turn.

SHAPE ROOF

Row 9 (RS) Ch 2, sl st in space in top of first scale, ch 3, dc in same sp as sl st, ch 2, *working through both thicknesses, work 2 dc between last and next scale and 2-dc group of row below, ch 2, work 2 dc in space in top of next scale, ch 2; rep from *, end join with a sl st in top left corner of scale below—nine 2-dc groups. Do not turn.

Row 10 (RS) Rep row 4, rep from * to * 4 times, end join with a sl st in top right corner of scale below—4 crocodile scales. Do not turn.

Row 11 (RS) Rep row 9—seven 2-dc groups. Do not turn.

Row 12 (RS) Rep row 4, rep from * to * 3 times, end join with a sl st in top right corner of scale below—3 crocodile scales. Fasten off, leaving a long tail for sewing.

FRONT OF HOUSE

With color B, ch 36.

Row 1 Sc in the 2nd ch from the hook and in each ch across—35 sc. Turn.

Rows 2–18 Ch 1, sc in each sc across. Turn. Fasten off, leaving a long tail for sewing.

BACK OF HOUSE

Work as for front of house.

DOOR

With color C, ch 6.

Row 1 Sc in the 2nd ch from the hook and in each ch across—5 sc. Turn.

Rows 2–7 Ch 1, sc in each sc across. Turn.

Row 8 Ch 1, skip first 2 sc, work 5 dc in the next sc, skip next sc, sl st in last sc. Fasten off, leaving a long tail for sewing.

WINDOW (MAKE 2)

With color D, ch 6.

Row 1 Sc in the 2nd ch from the hook and in each ch across—5 sc. Turn.

Rows 2–6 Ch 1, sc in each sc across. Turn. Fasten off, leaving a long tail for sewing.

WINDOW SHUTTER (MAKE 4)

With color C, ch 3.

Row 1 Sc in the 2nd ch from the hook and in each ch across—2 sc. Turn.

Rows 2–6 Ch 1, sc in each sc across. Turn. Fasten off, leaving a long tail for sewing.

LINING (MAKE 2)

With color B, ch 36.

Row 1 Sc in the 2nd ch from the hook and in each ch across—35 sc. Turn.

Rows 2–17 Ch 1, sc in each sc across. Turn.

Row 18 Ch 1, sc in each sc across, changing to A when completing last sc. Turn.

Rows 19–27 Ch 1, sc in each sc across. Turn.

Row 28 Ch 1, [sc2tog] twice, sc across next 27 sc, [sc2tog] twice—31 sc. Turn.

Row 29 Ch 1, [sc2tog] twice, sc across next 23 sc, [sc2tog] twice—27 sc. Turn.

Row 30 Ch 1, [sc2tog] twice, sc across next 19 sc, [sc2tog] twice—23 sc. Turn.

Row 31 Ch 1, [sc2tog] twice, sc across next 15 sc, [sc2tog] twice—19 sc. Turn.

Row 32 Ch 1, sc in each sc across. Turn.

Row 33 Ch 1, sc2tog, sc across next 15 sc, sc2tog—17 sc. Turn.

Row 34 Ch 1, sc2tog, sc across next 13 sc, sc2tog—15 sc. Turn.

Rows 35 and 36 Ch 1, sc in each sc across. Turn. Fasten off, leaving a long tail for sewing.

ASSEMBLY

1) Block roof pieces so crocodile scales lie flat.

2) Sew the top edge of the house front to the bottom edge of a roof piece. Repeat for the back of the house. Weave in ends and snip the excess.

3) For the doorknob, measure and mark with a straight pin, 1"/2.5cm from bottom edge of door and ⅜"/1cm from left-hand edge. Using color E, embroider a French knot doorknob, following the steps on page 22. Secure with a knot on the wrong side and weave in the ends.

4) Sew the door to the front of the house, one row up from the bottom edge and centered from side to side. Weave in ends and snip the excess.

5) For the window panes, use color E to embroider a vertical line of chain stitches up the center of each window; follow the steps for chain stitch on page 20. Embroider a horizontal line of chain stitches across the center of each window, then along top and bottom edges. Weave in ends and snip the excess.

6) Sew each window to the front of the house, 1¼"/3cm up from bottom edge and 2"/5cm from side edge. Weave in ends and snip the excess.

7) Sew the shutters onto each side of each window, overlapping them slightly onto the side edges of the windows. Weave in ends and snip the excess.

8) Using color A for the roof pieces and B for the house pieces, sew the house/roof pieces together, leaving the bottom edge open. Weave in ends and snip the excess. Turn right side out.

9) Using color A for the roof sections

I hope you enjoy making the roof as much as I did!

and B for the house sections, sew the lining pieces together, leaving the bottom edge open. Weave in ends and snip the excess. Leave wrong side out.

10) Insert the lining into house and sew the bottom edges together using B. Weave in ends and snip the excess. ◼

Diana Camera Purse

This charming camera bag pays homage to one of my favorite film cameras, a mint-green Diana Dreamer. The bag is the perfect size for plastic film cameras, film storage, point-and-shoot cameras, cell phones, and other essentials for anyone who likes to see the world through a camera lens!

FINISHED DIMENSIONS
CAMERA
Width 7"/17.5cm
Height 5"/12.5cm
Depth 3½"/9cm
STRAP
Width 1¾"/4.5cm
Length 38½"/97.5cm (excluding D-rings)

NOTES
1) When changing colors, draw new color through last 2 loops on hook to complete last stitch.
2) The strap is made by crocheting two separate pieces, then sewing them together.

BACK
With color A, ch 23.
Row 1 Sc in the 2nd ch from the hook and in each ch across—22 sc. Turn.
Rows 2–14 Ch 1, sc in each sc across. Turn.
Row 15 Ch 1, sc in each sc across, changing to color B. Turn.
Rows 16–20 Ch 1, sc in each sc. Turn. Fasten off, leaving a long tail for sewing.

FRONT
Work as for back.

SIDES (MAKE 2)
With color A, ch 11.
Row 1 Sc in the 2nd ch from the hook and in each ch across—10 sc. Turn.
Rows 2–14 Ch 1, sc in each sc across. Turn.
Row 15 Ch 1, sc in each sc across, changing to color B. Turn.
Rows 16–20 Ch 1, sc in each sc. Turn. Fasten off, leaving a long tail for sewing.

TOP (MAKE 2)
With color B, ch 23.
Row 1 Sc in the 2nd ch from the hook and in each ch across—22 sc. Turn.
Rows 2–6 Ch 1, sc in each sc across. Turn. Fasten off, leaving a long tail for sewing.

BOTTOM
With color A, ch 23.
Row 1 Sc in the 2nd ch from the hook and in each ch across—22 sc. Turn.
Rows 2–12 Ch 1, sc in each sc across. Turn. Fasten off, leaving a long tail for sewing.

LENS
With color C, ch 2.
Rnd 1 Work 6 sc in the 2nd ch from the hook, join rnd with a sl st in first sc.
Rnd 2 Ch 1, work 2 sc in same sc as joining, then work 2 sc in each rem sc

YARN
Super Value by Bernat, 7oz/198g, each approx 382yd/349m (acrylic); worsted weight

• 1 skein each in #8886 Mint (A), #07414 Natural (B), #07421 Black (C), #53044 True Grey (D), and #07391 White (E)

HOOK
• Size H/8 (5mm) crochet hook *or size to obtain gauge*

NOTIONS
• Two 1"/25mm nickel D-rings

• Two 2"/25mm nickel swivel hooks by Sewology

• One 7"/17.5cm polyester zipper in #256 Natural by Coats & Clark

• ½yd/.5m fabric for lining

• Sewing threads to match zipper and lining

• Sewing needle

• Straight pins

• Polyester fiberfill

GAUGE
12 sts and 16 rows = 4"/10cm over sc using size H/8 (5mm) hook.

Longtime blog readers might remember that Diana camera: it appeared in my header!

Diana Camera Purse

around, join rnd with a sl st in first sc—12 sc.

Rnd 3 Ch 1, work 2 sc in same sc as joining, sc in next sc, *work 2 sc in next sc, sc in next sc; rep from * around, join rnd with a sl st in first sc, changing to D—18 sc.

Rnd 4 Ch 1, work 2 sc in same sc as joining, sc in next 2 sc, *work 2 sc in next sc, sc in next 2 sc; rep from * around, join rnd with a sl st in first sc, changing to D—24 sc.

Rnd 5 Ch 1, work 2 sc in same sc as joining, sc in next 3 sc, *work 2 sc in next sc, sc in next 3 sc; rep from * around, join rnd with a sl st in first sc, changing to A—30 sc.

Rnd 6 Ch 1, working through back loops only, sc in same sc as joining, then sc in each rem sc around, join rnd with a sl st in first sc.

Rnds 7 and 8 Ch 1, sc in same sc as joining, then sc in each rem sc around. Fasten off, leaving a long tail for sewing.

VIEW FINDER

BACK

With color B, ch 6.

Row 1 Sc in the 2nd ch from the hook and in each ch across—5 sc. Turn.

Rows 2–5 Ch 1, sc in each sc across. Turn. Fasten off, leaving a long tail for sewing.

FRONT

With color E, ch 4.

Row 1 Sc in the 2nd ch from the hook and in each ch across—3 sc. Turn.

Rows 2 and 3 Ch 1, sc in each sc across. Turn. Fasten off, leaving a long tail for sewing.

STRAP (MAKE 2)

With color B, make a slip knot and place on the hook.

Row 1 Work 5 sc over the straight bar of a swivel hook. Turn.

Row 2 Ch 1, sc in each sc across. Turn. Rep row 2 until piece measures 38½"/97.5cm long (excluding swivel hook), or the desired length. Fasten off, leaving a tail long enough to sew one side edge of the strap.

D-RING TAB (MAKE 2)

With color A, make a slip knot and place on the hook.

Row 1 Work 5 sc over the straight bar of a D-ring. Turn.

Rows 2–4 Ch 1, sc in each sc across. Turn. Fasten off, leaving a long tail for sewing.

ASSEMBLY

1) For fabric lining, use crochet pieces as a guide and cut out fabric pieces ½"/1.5mm larger all around than the crochet pieces. Cut two backs (one will be the front), two sides, and one bottom.

2) With the right sides facing, pin front and back pieces to side pieces.

3) Beginning ½"/1.5mm from bottom edges, machine- or hand-stitch side seams using a ½"/1.5mm seam allowance.

4) Pin bottom piece to bottom edge of assembled pieces, then sew seam all around. Leave wrong side out. Set aside.

5) Following the instructions for chain stitch embroidery on page 20, embroider the 4-stitch highlight on the camera lens using E. Secure with a knot and weave in the ends.

6) Center the lens over the A section on the front. Sew in place and stuff the lens lightly with fiberfill before you finish sewing. Weave in the ends.

7) Sew the view finder front to the view finder back. Sew it to the B section on the front, above the camera lens.

8) Sew the front and back to the sides.

9) Sew on the bottom.

10) Position a D-ring tab on one side of purse, so first row of tab is even with last row of A and is centered side to side. Sew in place. Repeat on opposite side.

11) Sew the zipper to the two top pieces. Set aside.

12) Sew on the top.

13) Turn top edge of fabric lining ½"/1.5mm to wrong side. Insert lining into purse and sew top edge in place.

14) Place one strap on top of the other strap. On each side of the strap, have the top edge of last row of one strap just below the first row of the other strap. Sew edges together all around.

15) Hook the straps onto the D-rings. ■

Tablet Case

I keep my tablet with me wherever I go, using it to read craft magazines and books, watch TV shows, and keep up with social media. This case features a modern color palette, an extra pocket for your phone or cords, and a fabric lining for additional padding.

YARN
Sweater by Spud & Chloe, 3½oz/100g, each approx 160yd/146m (superwash wool/organic cotton); worsted weight

• 1 hank each in #7518 Barn (A), #7501 Popsicle (B), and #7519 Waterslide (C)

HOOKS
• Sizes G/6 and H/8 (4 and 5mm) crochet hooks *or size to obtain gauge*

NOTIONS
• One ¾"/19mm plastic button

• One 11½"/29cm x 17½"/44.5cm piece of fabric for lining

• Sewing thread to match lining

• Sewing needle

GAUGE
13 sts and 18 rows = 4"/10cm over sc using larger hook.

FINISHED DIMENSIONS
Width 10¼"/26cm
Length 8¼"/21cm

STITCH GLOSSARY
sc2tog [Insert hook in next sc, yo and draw up a loop] twice, yo and draw through all 3 loops on hook.

BACK
With larger hook and color A, ch 34.

Row 1 Sc in the 2nd ch from the hook and in each ch across—33 sc. Turn.
Rows 2–33 Ch 1, sc in each sc across. Turn.

FLAP
Rows 34–49 Ch 1, sc in each sc across. Turn. Fasten off and weave in the ends.

FRONT
With larger hook and color B, ch 34.

A tablet is a multitasker's best friend: I often watch TV shows while crocheting!

Tablet Case

Row 1 Sc in the 2nd ch from the hook and in each ch across—33 sc. Turn.
Rows 2–33 Ch 1, sc in each sc across. Turn. Fasten off and weave in the ends.

POCKET

With larger hook and color C, ch 25.
Row 1 Sc in the 2nd ch from the hook and in each ch across—24 sc. Turn.
Rows 2–21 Ch 1, sc in each sc across. Turn. Fasten off, leaving a long tail for sewing.

BUTTONHOLE PLACKET

With larger hook and color C, ch 11.
Row 1 Sc in the 2nd ch from the hook and in each ch across—10 sc. Turn.
Rows 2 and 3 Ch 1, sc in each sc across. Turn.
Row (buttonhole) 4 Ch 1, sc in the first 4 sc, ch 2, skip the next 2 sc, sc in the last 4 sc. Turn.
Row 5 Ch 1, sc in the first 4 sc, work 2 sc in ch-2 sp, sc in the last 4 sc. Turn.
Rows 6 and 7 Ch 1, sc in each sc across. Turn. Fasten off.

BUTTON

With smaller hook and color C, ch 2.
Rnd 1 Work 5 sc in the 2nd ch from hook, join rnd with a sl st in first sc.
Rnd 2 Ch 1, work 2 sc in each sc around, join rnd with a sl st in first sc—10 sc.
Rnd 3 Ch 1, sc in each sc around, join rnd with a sl st in first sc.

Rnd 4 Ch 1, [sc2tog] 5 times, inserting button before closing opening, join rnd with a sl st in first sc. Fasten off, leaving a long tail for sewing.

ASSEMBLY

1) Position the pocket on the back, so bottom and side edges of the pocket are 1½"/4cm from bottom and side edges of the back. Using the long tail of the pocket, sew the pocket in place, leaving the top edge open. Weave in the ends and snip the excess.
2) Position the front on the back, so bottom and side edges are even. Using the long tails, sew the front and back together, leaving the top edge of the front open. Weave in the ends and snip the excess.
3) Position the buttonhole placket on the flap, so top edge of buttonhole is even with bottom edge of flap and placket is centered side to side. Using the long tail, sew the placket in place. Weave in the ends and snip the excess.
4) Sew on the button.
5) For the lining, fold the lining fabric in half so right sides are facing. Hand- or machine-stitch a ½"/1.5cm seam along each side edge.
6) Fold the top edge of the lining ½"/1.5cm to the wrong side.
7) Insert the lining into the case. Whip stitch the top edge of the lining to the top edge of the front and along the same line across the back. ■

Gift Boxes
96
•
Crochet Latte
104
•
Blueberry
Muffin
107
•
Party Hat
Garland
110
•
Snow Cone
Garland
113
•
Crochet Edge
Cards and Tags
116

giving

Gift Boxes

Ready to try a new technique? These crochet gift boxes look like simple cubes made out of yarn, but they are actually strong enough to hold a gift inside. Soak the finished boxes (scary, I know!) in a sugar-water combination to create sturdy and special pieces.

Large Gift Box

FINISHED DIMENSIONS

BOX BOTTOM
5½" x 5½" x 5¼"/14cm x 14cm x 13.5cm
BOX LID
6" x 6" x 1¾"/15cm x 15cm x 4.5cm

STITCH GLOSSARY

FPdc (Front Post double crochet) Yo, insert hook from front to back around the post of the next stitch of the row below, yo and draw up a loop, [yo and draw through 2 loops on the hook] twice.

sc2tog [Insert hook in next sc, yo and draw up a loop] twice, yo and draw through all 3 loops on hook.

BOX BOTTOM

With color A, ch 4. Join with a slip stitch, forming a ring.

Rnd 1 Ch 3 (*never* counts as a dc), work 20 dc in the ring, join rnd with a sl st in first dc.

Rnd 2 Ch 3, dc in same dc as joining, dc in next 3 dc, work 5 dc in next dc (corner made), *dc in next 4 dc, work 5 dc in next dc; rep from * around twice more, join rnd with a sl st in first dc.

Rnd 3 Ch 3, dc in same dc as joining, dc in next 5 dc, work 5 dc in next dc, *dc in next 8 dc, work 5 dc in next dc; rep from * around twice more, end dc in last 2 dc, join rnd with a sl st in first dc.

Rnd 4 Ch 3, dc in same dc as joining, dc in next 7 dc, work 5 dc in next dc, *dc in next 12 dc, work 5 dc in next dc; rep from * around twice more, end dc in last 4 dc, join rnd with a sl st in first dc.

Rnd 5 Ch 1, working through back loops only for sc, sc in same dc as joining, sc in next 9 dc, FPdc around the next stitch of the rnd below, *sc in next 16 dc, FPdc around the next stitch of the rnd below; rep from * around twice more, end sc in last 6 dc, join rnd with a sl st in first sc. Continue to work through both loops as follows:

Rnds 6–14 Ch 3, dc in same stitch as joining, dc in next 9 dc, FPdc around the next stitch of the rnd below, *dc in next 16 dc, FPdc around the next stitch of the rnd below; rep from * around twice more, end dc in last 6 dc, join rnd with a sl st in first dc. Fasten off. Weave in ends.

BOX LID

With color A, ch 4. Join with a slip stitch, forming a ring. Repeat rnds 1–4 of box bottom.

LARGE GIFT BOX

YARN
Sweater by Spud & Chloë, 3½oz/100g, each approx 160yd/146m (superwash wool/organic cotton); worsted weight

- 2 hanks in #7513 Jelly Bean (A)

- 1 hank in #7518 Barn (B)

HOOK
- Size H/8 (5mm) crochet hook *or size to obtain gauge*

NOTIONS
- Safety pins

- Glass or enamel-lined saucepan

- 4 cups sugar

- Two large glass bowls

- Rubber gloves

- Large cardboard box

- Straight edge ruler

- Mat knife

- Cutting board

- Wide masking tape

- Aluminum foil

GAUGE
13 sts and 8 rnds = 4"/10cm over dc using size H/8 (5mm) hook.

Use the box to present a special gift to a friend, or as a holiday decoration at home!

Gift Boxes

Rnd 5 Ch 3, dc in same dc as joining, dc in next 9 dc, work 5 dc in next dc, *dc in next 16 dc, work 5 dc in next dc; rep from * around twice more, end dc in last 6 dc, join rnd with a sl st in first dc.

Rnd 6 Ch 1, working through back loops only for sc, sc in same dc as joining, sc in next 11 dc, FPdc around the next stitch of the rnd below, *sc in next 20 dc, FPdc around the next stitch of the rnd below; rep from * around twice more, end sc in last 8 dc, join rnd with a sl st in first sc. Continue to work through both loops as follows:

Rnds 7 and 8 Ch 3, dc in same stitch as joining, dc in next 11 dc, FPdc around the next stitch of the rnd below, *dc in next 20 dc, FPdc around the next stitch of the rnd below; rep from * around twice more, end dc in last 8 dc, join rnd with a sl st in first dc. Fasten off. Weave in ends.

BOW

With color B, ch 3.

Row 1 (RS) Sc in 2nd ch from hook and in each ch across—2 sc. Turn.

Rows 2–4 Ch 1, sc in each sc across. Turn.

Row 5 Ch 1, [2 sc in next sc] twice—4 sc. Turn.

Rows 6 and 7 Ch 1, sc in each sc across. Turn.

Row 8 Ch 1, sc in first sc, [work 2 sc in next sc] twice, sc in last sc—6 sc. Turn.

Rows 9–19 Ch 1, sc in each sc across. Turn.

Row 20 Ch 1, sc in first sc, [sc2tog] twice, sc in last sc—4 sc. Turn.

Rows 21 and 22 Ch 1, sc in each sc across. Turn.

Row 23 Ch 1, [sc2tog] twice—2 sc. Turn.

Rows 24–26 Ch 1, sc in each sc across. Turn.

Row 27 Ch 1, [2 sc in next sc] twice—4 sc. Turn.

Row 28 Ch 1, sc in each sc across. Turn.

Rows 29–50 Rep rows 5–26. Fasten off, leaving a long tail for sewing.

CENTER WRAP

With color B, ch 3.

Row 1 (RS) Sc in 2nd ch from hook and in each ch across—2 sc. Turn.

Rows 2–9 Ch 1, sc in each sc across. Turn. Fasten off, leaving a long tail for sewing.

LONG RIBBON PIECE

With color B, ch 4.

Row 1 (RS) Sc in 2nd ch from hook and in each ch across—3 sc. Turn.

Rows 2–33 Ch 1, sc in each sc across. Turn. Fasten off, leaving a long tail for sewing.

SHORT RIBBON PIECE (MAKE 2)

With color B, ch 4.

Row 1 (RS) Sc in 2nd ch from hook and in each ch across—3 sc. Turn.

Rows 2–15 Ch 1, sc in each sc across. Turn. Fasten off, leaving a long tail for sewing.

ASSEMBLY

1) Position the long ribbon piece over the box lid, so ends are even with bottom edge of lid and are centered side to side. Pin to secure, then sew in place. Weave in ends and snip the excess.

2) Position the short ribbon pieces over the box lid, so top edges butt the long ribbon piece, bottom edges are even with bottom edge of lid, and both are centered side to side. Pin to secure, then sew in place. Weave in ends and snip the excess.

3) To make the bow, sew the first row to the last row, forming a circle.

4) Center the seam over the center of the bow, then wrap the center of the bow with the center wrap.

5) Sew the first and last row of the center wrap together, then bring the yarn up through the center of the bow and back down through the bottom to secure the wrap in place.

6) Sew the bow to the center of the lid as shown. Weave in ends and snip the excess.

CARDBOARD BOX MOLDS AND DRYING RACKS

1) From the cardboard box, fashion a 5" x 5" x 5"/12.5cm x 12.5cm x 12.5cm box bottom, and a 5⅜" x

5⅜" x 1½"/13.5cm x 13.5cm x 4cm box lid. Use masking tape to hold pieces together.

2) Cover the outside of the box bottom and lid very neatly with aluminum foil. Wrap the foil over the edge, taking care that the foil is smooth and flat. Secure foil edges with masking tape.

3) For the drying racks, cut two 12"/30.5cm squares from cardboard. Wrap squares with foil, securing edges in place with masking tape.

SUGAR WATER STIFFENING

1) Place 4 cups of sugar and 4 cups of cold tap water into the pot. Stir well and bring the liquid to a boil. Remove the pot from the stove and let the mixture cool. Pour mixture into a large bowl.

2) Wearing rubber gloves, immerse the pieces into the sugar-water mixture and allow the liquid to soak through the fabric for about 15 minutes.

3) Place the foil-covered box and box lid on top of the foil-wrapped racks.

4) Place the soaked pieces inside the empty bowl. Press each piece against the sides of the bowl to remove excess liquid. Do NOT twist or wring out.

5) Position the crochet box bottom over the cardboard box bottom, lining up corners and top edges. Place box top edge down on the rack.

Gift Boxes

6) For box lid, repeat step 5, then place lid bottom edge down on the rack.

7) For each bow loop, tear a piece of aluminum foil. Form into a round tube and slide it in the middle of the bow loop to keep loop open.

8) Allow the box and lid to dry completely in a cool place, preferably near a fan, for five to seven days.

9) Once the box pieces are completely dry, remove cardboard molds.

10) Place the lid on top of the box. ■

Small Gift Box

Here's a smaller version of the gift box—make a few in different sizes and arrange them into a festive display for the holidays, or use them as décor at a bridal or baby shower or a birthday party!

FINISHED DIMENSIONS
BOX BOTTOM
4½" x 4½" x 4⅜"/11.5cm x 11.5cm x 11cm
BOX LID
5" x 5" x 1¾"/12.5cm x 12.5cm x 4.5cm

STITCH GLOSSARY
FPdc (Front Post double crochet)
Yo, insert hook from front to back around the post of the next stitch of the row below, yo and draw up a loop, [yo and draw through 2 loops on the hook] twice.

sc2tog [Insert hook in next sc, yo and draw up a loop] twice, yo and draw through all 3 loops on hook.

BOX BOTTOM
With color A, ch 4. Join with a slip stitch, forming a ring.

Rnd 1 Ch 3 (*never* counts as a dc), work 20 dc in the ring, join rnd with a sl st in first dc.

Rnd 2 Ch 3, dc in same dc as joining, dc in next 3 dc, work 5 dc in next dc (corner made), *dc in next 4 dc, work 5 dc in next dc; rep from * around twice more, join rnd with a sl st in first dc.

Rnd 3 Ch 3, dc in same dc as joining, dc in next 5 dc, work 5 dc in next dc, *dc in next 8 dc, work 5 dc in next dc; rep from * around twice more, end dc in last 2 dc, join rnd with a sl st in first dc.

Rnd 4 Ch 1, working through back loops only for sc, sc in same dc as joining, sc in next 7 dc, FPdc around the next stitch of the rnd below, *sc in next 12 dc, FPdc around the next stitch of the rnd below; rep from * around twice more, end sc in last 4 dc, join rnd with a sl st in first sc. Continue to work through both loops as follows:

Rnds 5–12 Ch 3, dc in same stitch as joining, dc in next 7 dc, FPdc around

SMALL BOX

YARN
Sweater by Spud & Chloë, 3½oz/100g, each approx 160yd/146m (superwash wool/organic cotton); worsted weight

• 1 hank each in #7519 Waterslide (A) and #7510 Splash (B)

HOOK
• Size H/8 (5mm) crochet hook *or size to obtain gauge*

NOTIONS
• Safety pins

• Glass or enamel-lined saucepan

• 4 cups sugar

• Two large glass bowls

• Rubber gloves

• Large cardboard box

• Straight edge ruler

• Mat knife

• Cutting board

• Wide masking tape

• Aluminum foil

GAUGE
13 sts and 8 rnds = 4"/10cm over dc using size H/8 (5mm) hook.

A few of these boxes would make a charming centerpiece for your holiday table!

Gift Boxes

the next stitch of the rnd below, *dc in next 12 dc, FPdc around the next stitch of the rnd below; rep from * around twice more, end dc in last 4 dc, join rnd with a sl st in first dc. Fasten off. Weave in ends.

BOX LID

With color A, ch 4. Join with a slip stitch, forming a ring. Repeat rnds 1–3 of box bottom.

Rnd 4 Ch 3, dc in same dc as joining, dc in next 7 dc, work 5 dc in next dc, *dc in next 12 dc, work 5 dc in next dc; rep from * around twice more, end dc in last 4 dc, join rnd with a sl st in first dc.

Rnd 5 Ch 1, working through back loops only for sc, sc in same dc as joining, sc in next 9 dc, FPdc around the next stitch of the rnd below, *sc in next 16 dc, FPdc around the next stitch of the rnd below; rep from * around twice more, end sc in last 6 dc, join rnd with a sl st in first sc. Continue to work through both loops as follows:

Rnds 6 and 7 Ch 3, dc in same stitch as joining, dc in next 9 dc, FPdc around the next stitch of the rnd below, *dc in next 16 dc, FPdc around the next stitch of the rnd below; rep from * around twice more, end dc in last 6 dc, join rnd with a sl st in first dc. Fasten off. Weave in ends.

BOW

With color B, ch 3.

Row 1 (RS) Sc in 2nd ch from hook and in each ch across—2 sc. Turn.

Rows 2 and 3 Ch 1, sc in each sc across. Turn.

Row 4 Ch 1, [2 sc in next sc] twice—4 sc. Turn.

Rows 5–7 Ch 1, sc in each sc across. Turn.

Row 8 Ch 1, sc in first sc, [work 2 sc in next sc] twice, sc in last sc—6 sc. Turn.

Rows 9–16 Ch 1, sc in each sc across. Turn.

Row 17 Ch 1, sc in first sc, [sc2tog] twice, sc in last sc—4 sc. Turn.

Rows 18–20 Ch 1, sc in each sc across. Turn.

Row 21 Ch 1, [sc2tog] twice—2 sc. Turn.

Rows 22–24 Ch 1, sc in each sc across. Turn.

Rows 25–44 Rep rows 4–23. Fasten off, leaving a long tail for sewing.

CENTER WRAP

With color B, ch 3.

Row 1 (RS) Sc in 2nd ch from hook and in each ch across—2 sc. Turn.

Rows 2–9 Ch 1, sc in each sc across. Turn. Fasten off, leaving a long tail for sewing.

LONG RIBBON PIECE

With color B, ch 4.

Row 1 (RS) Sc in 2nd ch from hook and in each ch across—3 sc. Turn.

Rows 2–31 Ch 1, sc in each sc across. Turn. Fasten off, leaving a long tail for sewing.

SHORT RIBBON PIECE (MAKE 2)

With color B, ch 4.

Row 1 (RS) Sc in 2nd ch from hook and in each ch across—3 sc. Turn.

Rows 2–15 Ch 1, sc in each sc across. Turn. Fasten off, leaving a long tail for sewing.

ASSEMBLY

Work steps 1–6 as for large box.

CARDBOARD BOX MOLDS AND DRYING RACKS

1) From the cardboard box, fashion a 4" x 4" x 4"/10cm x 10cm x 10cm box bottom, and a 4½" x 4½" x 1½" x 1½"/11.5cm x 11.5cm x 4cm box lid. Use masking tape to hold pieces together.

2) Cover the outside of the box bottom and lid very neatly with aluminum foil. Wrap the foil over the edge, taking care that the foil is smooth and flat. Secure foil edges with masking tape.

3) For the drying racks, cut two 12"/30.5cm squares from cardboard. Wrap squares with foil, securing edges in place with masking tape.

SUGAR WATER STIFFENING

Work steps 1–10 as for large box. ■

Crochet Latte

Crochet this latte to go with the blueberry muffin on page 107! Include a gift card to a local coffee shop, and give the set as a gift to a loved one who appreciates good food and creative crafting.

FINISHED MEASUREMENTS
Upper circumference 10½"/26.5cm
Height 4¼"/10.5cm

CUP
With color A, ch 2.

Rnd 1 Work 6 sc in the 2nd ch from the hook. Do not join. Mark the last stitch made with the stitch marker or safety pin. You will be working in a spiral, marking the last stitch made with the stitch marker or safety pin to indicate end of rnd.

Rnd 2 Work 2 sc in each sc around—12 sc.

Rnd 3 *Work 2 sc in next sc, sc in next sc; rep from * around—18 sc.

Rnd 4 *Work 2 sc in next sc, sc in next 2 sc; rep from * around—24 sc.

Rnd 5 Working through back loops only, sc in each stitch around.

Rnds 6–11 Sc in each sc around.

Rnd 12 *Work 2 sc in next sc, sc in next 3 sc; rep from * around—30 sc.

Rnds 13–17 Sc in each sc around.

Rnd 18 *Work 2 sc in next sc, sc in next 4 sc; rep from * around—36 sc.

Rnds 19–21 Sc in each sc around. Fasten off. Weave in the ends.

LATTE
With color B, ch 2.

Rnd 1 Work 6 sc in the 2nd ch from the hook. Do not join. Mark the last stitch made with the stitch marker or safety pin. You will be working in a spiral, marking the last stitch made with the stitch marker or safety pin to indicate end of rnd.

Rnd 2 Work 2 sc in each sc around—12 sc.

Rnd 3 *Work 2 sc in next sc, sc in next sc; rep from * around—18 sc.

Rnd 4 *Work 2 sc in next sc, sc in next 2 sc; rep from * around—24 sc.

Rnd 5 *Work 2 sc in next sc, sc in next 3 sc; rep from * around—30 sc.

Rnd 6 *Work 2 sc in next sc, sc in next 4 sc; rep from * around—36 sc. Fasten off, leaving a long tail for sewing.

PAPER SLEEVE
With color C, ch 8.

Row 1 Sc in the 2nd ch from the hook and in each ch across—7 sc. Turn.

Row 2 Ch 1, sc in each sc across. Turn. Rep row 2 until piece measures 8½"/21.5cm from beg. Fasten off, leaving a long tail for sewing.

YARN
Super Value by Bernat, 7oz/198g, each approx 382yd/349m (acrylic); medium worsted weight

• 1 skein each in #07391 White (A), #07469 Honey (B), and #53201 Aqua (C)

HOOK
• Size H/8 (5mm) crochet hook *or size to obtain gauge*

NOTIONS
• Removable stitch marker or small safety pin

• Polyester fiberfill

• Tracing paper

GAUGE
14 sts and 20 rnds = 4"/10cm over sc using size H/8 (5mm) hook.

The latte art embroidery template can be found on page 106.

Crochet Latte

LATTE ART DESIGN

1) Trace the latte art design on page 106 on the tracing paper.

2) Leave a ½"/13mm border all around and cut out the design.

3) Following the instructions for chain stitch embroidery on page 20, embroider the latte art design on top of the latte circle using A. Secure with a knot and weave in the ends.

ASSEMBLY

1) Position the sleeve in the middle of the cup. Sew all the way around the top and bottom edge of the sleeve to secure it in place. Weave in the ends.

2) Stuff the latte cup firmly with fiberfill.

3) Place the latte circle on top of the cup and sew it to the inside edge of the cup. Before you close the opening, make sure the latte has enough stuffing inside. Finish sewing and weave in the ends. ■

Blueberry Muffin

Invite your friends on a never-ending coffee date! Crochet an adorable blueberry muffin as a sweet reminder of times spent with friends, sipping coffee and sharing life stories.

YARN
Super Value by Bernat, 7oz/198g, each approx 382yd/349m (acrylic); worsted weight

• 1 skein each in #53010 Oatmeal (A), #08879 Sky (B), and #00616 Peacock (C)

HOOK
• Size H/8 (5mm) crochet hook or size to *obtain gauge*

NOTIONS
• Removable stitch marker or small safety pin

• Polyester fiberfill

GAUGE
14 sts and 20 rnds = 4"/10cm over sc using size H/8 (5mm) hook.

Place the muffin inside the wrapper and imagine the sweet scent of blueberries!

FINISHED DIMENSIONS

MUFFIN
Circumference 8¾"/22cm
Height 2¾"/7cm
MUFFIN WRAPPER
Circumference 9"/23cm
Height 2"/5cm

STITCH GLOSSARY

sc2tog [Insert hook in next sc, yo and draw up a loop] twice, yo and draw through all 3 loops on hook.

MUFFIN TOP

With color A, ch 2.
Rnd 1 Work 6 sc in the 2nd ch from the hook. Do not join. Mark the last stitch made with the stitch marker or safety pin. You will be working in a spiral, marking the last stitch made with the stitch marker or safety pin to indicate end of rnd.
Rnd 2 Work 2 sc in each sc around—12 sc.
Rnd 3 *Work 2 sc in next sc, sc in next sc; rep from * around—18 sc.

Blueberry Muffin

Rnd 4 *Work 2 sc in next sc, sc in next 2 sc; rep from * around—24 sc.
Rnd 5 *Work 2 sc in next sc, sc in next 3 sc; rep from * around—30 sc.
Rnds 6 and 7 Sc in each sc around.
Rnd 8 *Sc2tog, sc in the next 3 sc; rep from * around—24 sc. Fasten off, leaving a long tail for sewing.

MUFFIN BOTTOM

With color A, ch 2. Rep rnds 1–4 as for muffin top—24 sc.
Rnd 5 Working through back loops only, sc in each stitch around.
Rnds 6–8 Sc in each sc around. Join last rnd with a sl st. Fasten off, leaving a long tail for sewing.

BLUEBERRIES

1) For blueberries, cut a long length of color C. Tie a knot at one end and thread it through a tapestry needle.

2) Bring the yarn up through the top of the muffin top, from wrong side to right side. Embroider French knots in various spots on the top of the muffin. Follow the steps to make a French knot on page 22. Secure with a knot in the back and weave in the ends.

MUFFIN ASSEMBLY

1) Stuff the top and bottom of the muffin firmly with fiberfill.
2) Thread the long tail on the muffin base through the tapestry needle. Sew the bottom of the muffin to the top of the muffin. Before you close the muffin all the way, make sure it has enough fiberfill inside.
3) Weave in the ends and snip the excess.

MUFFIN WRAPPER SIDES

With color B, ch 8.
Row 1 Sc in the 2nd ch from the hook and in each ch across—7 sc. Turn.

Row 2 Ch 1, working through back loops only, sc in each stitch across. Turn.
Rows 3–30 Rep row 2. Fasten off, leaving a long tail for sewing.

MUFFIN WRAPPER BOTTOM

With color B, ch 2. Rep rnds 1–4 as for muffin top, joining last rnd with a sl st. Fasten off, leaving a long tail for sewing.

MUFFIN WRAPPER ASSEMBLY

1) Thread the long tail of the wrapper sides through a tapestry needle. Sew the first row to the last row, joining the piece together to form a circle. Weave in the ends and snip the excess.
2) Sew the muffin wrapper bottom to the bottom edge of the wrapper sides. Weave in the ends and snip the excess. ■

Party Hat Garland

Celebrate someone's special day with a cheerful crochet party hat garland—you can vary the colors to include the guest of honor's favorites. This garland makes a great decoration and a memorable keepsake!

FINISHED DIMENSIONS
Width 4½"/11.5cm
Length 5"/12.5cm

NOTE
When changing colors, draw new color through last 2 loops on hook to complete last stitch.

PLAIN PARTY HAT
(MAKE 2)
With color A, ch 2.
Rnd 1 Work 4 sc in the 2nd ch from the hook. Do not join. Mark the last stitch made with the stitch marker or safety pin. You will be working in a spiral, marking the last stitch made with the stitch marker or safety pin to indicate end of rnd.
Rnd 2 Sc in each sc around.
Rnd 3 Work 2 sc in each sc around—8 sc.
Rnds 4 and 5 Sc in each sc around.
Rnd 6 *Sc in next sc, work 2 sc in next sc; rep from * around—12 sc.
Rnd 7 Sc in each sc around.
Rnd 8 *Sc in next 2 sc, work 2 sc in next sc; rep from * around—16 sc.

Rnds 9 and 10 Sc in each sc around.
Rnd 11 *Sc in next 3 sc, work 2 sc in next sc; rep from * around—20 sc.
Rnd 12 Sc in each sc around.
Rnd 13 *Sc in next 4 sc, work 2 sc in next sc; rep from * around—24 sc.
Rnds 14 and 15 Sc in each sc around.
Rnd 16 *Sc in next 5 sc, work 2 sc in next sc; rep from * around—28 sc.
Rnd 17 Sc in each sc around.
Rnd 18 *Sc in next 6 sc, work 2 sc in next sc; rep from * around, changing to color B—32 sc.
Rnd 19 Sc in each sc around.
Rnd 20 *Sc in next 7 sc, work 2 sc in next sc; rep from * around—36 sc. Fasten off. Weave in the ends.

POLKA DOT PARTY HAT
(MAKE 3)
With color C, work as for plain party hat to rnd 17. Change to color D on rnd 18. Continue to work as for plain party hat.

POLKA DOT (MAKE 18)
With color B, ch 2.
Rnd 1 Work 4 sc in the 2nd ch from the hook. Join rnd with a sl st. Fasten off, leaving a long tail for sewing.

YARN
Sweater by Spud & Chloë, 3½oz/100g, each approx 160yd/146m (superwash wool/ organic cotton); worsted weight

• 1 hank each in #7519 Waterslide (A) and #7502 Grass (B), #7510 Splash (C) and #7513 Jellybean (D)

• Small amount of #7500 Ice Cream for garland string

HOOK
• Size H/8 (5mm) crochet hook

NOTIONS
• Pom-pom maker

• Removable stitch marker or small safety pin

GAUGE
Gauge is not important for this project.

Think about other cute items—like the snow cones on page 113—to make into garlands!

Party Hat Garland

POM-POM

Following pom-pom maker instructions, use color B to make two 1¾"/4.5cm diameter pom-poms for plain party hat and use color D to make three for polka dot party hat.

ASSEMBLY

1) Sew pom-poms onto hats, using same color yarn as pom-poms.
2) Sew six polka dots onto each polka dot party hat in a random pattern.
3) Weave in ends and snip the excess.
4) Thread a long length of Ice Cream in a tapestry needle. Draw the yarn through the top of each hat. ■

Snow Cone Garland

Who doesn't love snow cones? I transformed my favorite summertime treat into a charming party decoration. This crochet garland is perfect to hang above the treats table at your next gathering—have fun celebrating underneath it!

YARN
Sweater by Spud & Chloë, 3½oz/100g, each approx 160yd/146m (superwash wool/ organic cotton); worsted weight

• 1 hank each in #7500 Ice Cream (A), #7513 Jellybean (B), #7528 Life Jacket (C), #7505 Firefly (D), #7502 Grass (E), and #7519 Waterslide (F)

HOOK
• Size H/8 (5mm) crochet hook

NOTIONS
• Removable stitch marker or small safety pin

• Polyester fiberfill

GAUGE
Gauge is not important for this project.

Decorate the cake for your party to match the colors in the garland!

FINISHED DIMENSIONS
Before stuffing
Width 3½"/9cm
Length 5"/12.5cm

CONE PAPER CUP (MAKE 5)
With color A, ch 2.
Rnd 1 Work 4 sc in the 2nd ch from the hook. Do not join. Mark the last stitch made with the stitch marker or safety pin.

You will be working in a spiral, marking the last stitch made with the stitch marker or safety pin to indicate end of rnd.
Rnd 2 Sc in each sc around.
Rnd 3 Work 2 sc in each sc around—8 sc.
Rnds 4 and 5 Sc in each sc around.
Rnd 6 *Sc in next sc, work 2 sc in next sc; rep from * around—12 sc.
Rnd 7 Sc in each sc around.

Snow Cone Garland

Rnd 8 *Sc in next 2 sc, work 2 sc in next sc; rep from * around—16 sc.

Rnd 9 Sc in each sc around.

Rnd 10 *Sc in next 3 sc, work 2 sc in next sc; rep from * around—20 sc.

Rnd 11 Sc in each sc around.

Rnd 12 *Sc in next 4 sc, work 2 sc in next sc; rep from * around—24 sc.

Rnd 13 Sc in each sc around.

Rnd 14 *Sc in next 5 sc, work 2 sc in next sc; rep from * around—28 sc. Fasten off. Weave in the ends.

SNOW CONE FLAVOR (MAKE 5)

With color B, ch 2.

Rnd 1 Work 4 sc in the 2nd ch from the hook. Do not join. Mark the last stitch made with the stitch marker or safety pin. You will be working in a spiral, marking the last stitch made with the stitch marker or safety pin to indicate end of rnd.

Rnd 2 Work 2 sc in each sc around—8 sc.

Rnd 3 *Sc in next sc, work 2 sc in next sc; rep from * around—12 sc.

Rnd 4 *Sc in next 2 sc, work 2 sc in next sc; rep from * around—16 sc.

Rnd 5 *Sc in next 3 sc, work 2 sc in next sc; rep from * around—20 sc.

Rnd 6 *Sc in next 4 sc, work 2 sc in next sc; rep from * around—24 sc.

Rnd 7 *Sc in next 5 sc, work 2 sc in next sc; rep from * around—28 sc. Fasten off, leaving a long tail for sewing. Make 4 more using C, D, E, and F.

ASSEMBLY

1) Stuff the cone paper cup with fiberfill.

2) Place one of the snow cone flavor pieces on top of the cone paper cup. Use the long tail to sew the flavor to the inside edge of the cup. Before you finishing sewing it closed, stuff firmly with fiberfill to give the snow cone its shape.

3) Weave in ends and snip the excess.

4) Thread a long length of color A in a tapestry needle. Draw the yarn through the top section of each cone paper cup. ■

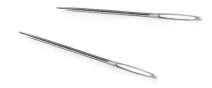

Crochet Edge Cards and Tags

One of the best feelings is the world is receiving a thoughtful letter from a friend—and a crochet edge makes snail mail even more personal. My talented friend Oana Befort illustrated the cards and tags shown here, which are also pictured on pages 116–121.

FINISHED DIMENSIONS
CARD
5¼" x 7"/13.5cm x 18cm
GIFT TAG
2¾" x 4"/7cm x 10cm

CARD
Print and cut out the card. Punch a hole through each dot marked on the card.

CROCHET EDGING
Using desired color, make a slip knot and place on the hook. With front side of card facing, insert hook into any corner hole, then join yarn with a sl st in hole.
Rnd 1 (RS) Ch 3, *sl st in next hole, ch 3; rep from * to next corner hole, work (sl st, ch 3, sl st) in corner hole; rep from * around to beginning corner hole, end sl st in beginning corner hole, ch 3, join rnd with a sl st in top of beginning ch-3.
Rnd 2 *Work (sc, 3 hdc, sc) in next ch-3 sp; rep from * around, join rnd with a sl st in first sc. Fasten off. Weave in ends and snip the excess.

GIFT TAG
Print and cut out the gift tag. Punch a hole through each dot marked on the tag. Continue to work as for cards. Cut a length of yarn in a matching color and tie it to the left edge of the crocheted edging. Attach the gift tag to your present and secure with a knot. Snip the excess yarn. ■

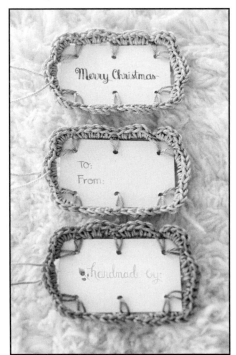

YARN
Egyptian Cotton DK by Sublime, 1¾oz/50g, each approx 115yd/105m (cotton); DK weight

• 1 ball each in #324 Rush Hour, #329 Cornelia, and #328 Freya

HOOK
• Size E/4 (3.5mm) crochet hook

NOTIONS
• Printable 4½" x 5"/ 11.5cm x 12.5cm cards and 1⅞" x 2⅞"/ 4.5cm x 7.5cm gift tags designed by Oana Befort

• Hole punch

• Scissors

GAUGE
Gauge is not important for this project.

Attach crocheted tags to all your gifts for a special handmade touch!

Crochet Edge Cards and Tags

To print these images at the size given in the pattern, enlarge the cards by 175% and the tags by 135%.

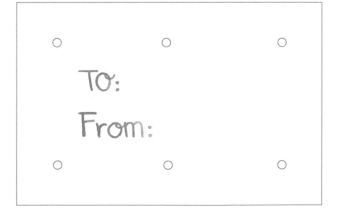

Crochet Edge Cards and Tags

You can also use your own artwork or commission some from your favorite local artists—such as your kids!

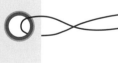

Facts & Figures

ABBREVIATIONS

approx   approximately

beg   begin; beginning; begins

BPdc   back post double crochet

ch   chain; chains

cl   cluster

cont   continue; continuing

dc   double crochet

dec   decrease; decreasing

dtr   double treble crochet

foll   follow(s) (ing)

FPdc   front post double crochet

grp(s)   group(s)

hdc   half double crochet

inc   increase; increasing

lp(s)   loop(s)

pat(s)   pattern(s)

RS   right side

rem   remain(s) (ing)

rep   repeat

reverse sc   reverse single crochet (aka crab stitch)

rnd(s)   round(s)

sc   single crochet

sc2tog   single crochet two together

sk   skip

sl   slip; slipping

sl st   slip stitch

sp(s)   space(s)

st(s)   stitch(es)

tbl   through back loop

t-ch   turning chain

tfl   through front loop

tog   together

tr   treble crochet

trtr   triple treble crochet

WS   wrong side

work even   continue in pattern without increasing or decreasing (U.K.: work straight)

yo   yarn over—making a new stitch by wrapping the yarn around the hook (U.K.: yoh)

( )   work instructions contained inside the parentheses into the stitch indicated

[ ]   rep instructions within brackets as many times as directed

*   rep instructions following an asterisk as many times as indicated

CONVERSION CHART

U.S. TERM	U.K./AUS. TERM
sl st (slip stitch)	**sc** (single crochet)
sc (single crochet)	**dc** (double crochet)
hdc (half double crochet)	**htr** (half treble crochet)
dc (double crochet)	**tr** (treble crochet)
tr (treble crochet)	**dtr** (double treble crochet)
dtr (double treble crochet)	**trip tr or trtr** (triple treble crochet)
trtr (triple treble crochet)	**qtr** (quadruple treble crochet)
rev sc (reverse single crochet)	**rev dc** (reverse double crochet)
yo (yarn over)	**yoh** (yarn over hook)

STANDARD YARN WEIGHT SYSTEM

Categories of yarn, gauge ranges, and recommended needle and hook sizes

Yarn Weight Symbol & Category Names	0 Lace	1 Super Fine	2 Fine	3 Light	4 Medium	5 Bulky	6 Super Bulky
Type of Yarns in Category	Fingering 10 count crochet thread	Sock, Fingering, Baby	Sport, Baby	DK, Light Worsted	Worsted, Afghan, Aran	Chunky, Craft, Rug	Bulky, Roving
Knit Gauge Range* in Stockinette Stitch to 4 inches	33–40** sts	27–32 sts	23–26 sts	21–24 sts	16–20 sts	12–15 sts	6–11 sts
Recommended Needle in Metric Size Range	1.5–2.25 mm	2.25–3.25 mm	3.25–3.75 mm	3.75–4.5 mm	4.5–5.5 mm	5.5–8 mm	8 mm and larger
Recommended Needle U.S. Size Range	000 to 1	1 to 3	3 to 5	5 to 7	7 to 9	9 to 11	11 and larger
Crochet Gauge* Ranges in Single Crochet to 4 inch	32-42 double crochets**	21–32 sts	16–20 sts	12–17 sts	11–14 sts	8–11 sts	5–9 sts
Recommended Hook in Metric Size Range	Steel*** 1.6–1.4mm Regular hook 2.25 mm	2.25–3.5 mm	3.5–4.5 mm	4.5–5.5 mm	5.5–6.5 mm	6.5–9 mm	9 mm and larger
Recommended Hook U.S. Size Range	Steel*** 6, 7, 8 Regular hook B–1	B–1 to E–4	E–4 to 7	7 to I–9	I–9 to K–10½	K–10½ to M–13	M–13 and larger

* GUIDELINES ONLY: The above reflect the most commonly used gauges and needle or hook sizes for specific yarn categories.

** Lace weight yarns are usually knitted or crocheted on larger needles and hooks to create lacy openwork patterns. Accordingly, a gauge range is difficult to determine. Always follow the gauge stated in your pattern.

*** Steel crochet hooks are sized differently from regular hooks—the higher the number, the smaller the hook, which is the reverse of regular hook sizing.

This Standards & Guidelines booklet and downloadable symbol artwork are available at: YarnStandards.com

CROCHET HOOKS

U.S.	METRIC
B/1	2.25mm
C/2	2.75mm
D/3	3.25mm
E/4	3.5mm
F/5	3.75mm
G/6	4mm
7	4.5mm
H/8	5mm
I/9	5.5mm
J/10	6mm
K/10½	6.5mm
L/11	8mm
M/13	9mm
N/15	10mm

Resources

AUNT LYDIA'S
A Coats & Clark Brand

BERNAT YARNS
A division of Spinrite LP
320 Livingstone Avenue South
Box 40
Listowel, ON
Canada
N4W 3H3
www.yarnspirations.com/bernat

COATS & CLARK
PO Box 12229
Greenville, SC 29612
Tel: (800) 648-1479
www.coatsandclark.com

DEBBIE BLISS
Distributed by Knitting Fever
www.debbieblissonline.com

HOBBY LOBBY STORES, INC.
7707 S.W. 44th Street
Oklahoma City, OK 73179
www.hobbylobby.com

KNITTING FEVER (KFI)
PO Box 336
315 Bayview Avenue
Amityville, NY 11701
www.knittingfever.com

ROWAN YARNS
Green Lane Mill
Holmfirth, West Yorkshire
HD9 2DX
England
Tel.: +44 (0)1484 681881
www.knitrowan.com

SPUD & CHLOË
Blue Sky Alpacas
Attn: Spud & Chloë
PO Box 88
Cedar, MN 55011
Tel: (888) 460-8862
www.spudandchloe.com

SUBLIME YARNS
A division of Sirdar Spinning Ltd.
Flanshaw Lane Alverthorpe
Wakefield
WF2 9ND
United Kingdom
Tel.: +44 (0)1924 369666
sublimeyarns.com

If you want to see more of the beautiful illustrations featured throughout this book, including the gift cards and tags pictured on pages 116–121, visit Oanabefort.com.

Acknowledgments

This book would exist only as scribbles in my notebook without the amazing colleagues, friends, and family who supported me throughout the process. I am a big fan of thank-you notes, so let's call this my "Thank You" card to everyone who supported me, hugged me, prayed over me, cheered me on, celebrated with me, and often believed in me more than I believed in myself.

I created this book with the hope that it would glorify God and honor the creative abilities He has given me. It is because of Him that I have the ability to express myself in this way, and I can only hope to continue doing so for the rest of my life.

In July 2012 I came to Trisha Malcolm's office at Soho Publishing/ Sixth&Spring Books hoping for a job offer. Instead she asked me a very surprising question: "Are you interested in writing a book?" Thank you, Trisha, for believing in my work and giving me this amazing opportunity to become an author!

Thank you to Joy Aquilino, my first editor, who was so patient and helpful as I learned the ins and outs of writing a book. Your guidance and encouragement meant the world to me.

Lisa Silverman took over the project for the last few months: thank you, Lisa, for all your hard work! I also want to thank the many companies who donated their beautiful yarns.

The amazing photography is by the supremely talented Kelly Musgraves. The moment I realized I needed a photographer, she came to mind, and when I presented the project to her she was excited about working together. Kelly, I am thankful that I was lucky enough to work alongside you and create beautiful images together.

It was an honor to work with the amazingly talented Oana Befort on the illustrations. Her artwork is breathtaking—and she has the coolest name ever! Thank you, Oana, for creating illustrations that fit my style and adding a beautiful element to the book.

Thank you to the lovely Chantal Hickman for doing makeup. You are a true artist! I am so happy I met you through this project. I also want to thank Madison McDaniel, Abbie Mahoney, and Lauren Hall for modeling my creations. You three are beautiful inside and out. Thank you to the stylists of Pouf Blowout for styling the models' hair!

My mom and dad are the greatest parents in the world. This book would not have happened without their support, encouragement, and love. They believed in my dreams before I was born, and I know they will always be by my side. I love you both very much!

My dear friend Leilani Dodgen is the one who originally encouraged me to start a blog about my passion for yarn. Thank you, Leilani, for pushing me toward something that seemed terrifying but eventually helped me start letting go of my fears.

Thank you to my friends, who believed in me every step of the way, from the moment I announced the news to the day I held the finished book in my hands. I am blessed to have the support of so many amazing women.

Last but not least, I want to thank every single person who reads my blog. Whether you've been around from the beginning or are just now typing "One Sheepish Girl" into Google, thank you for your spreading the word about my site, leaving kind comments, taking the time to email me words of encouragement, and making One Sheepish Girl what it is today. ∎

Index

A

abbreviations 122
accessories
    Bow Brooch 36–41
    Color Block Ribbed Turban 34–35
Diana Camera Purse 26, 88–90
Granny Square Infinity Cowl 30–33
    Heart Pocket Apron 72–75
    Scallop Stripe Cowl 48–49
    Stripe Bow Clutch 38–41

B

basic crochet stitches 13–27
blocking, spray 24
Blueberry Muffin 107–109
Bow Brooch 36–41

C

chain stitch 20–21
Collared Shirt Makeover 45–47
Color Block Ribbed Turban 34–35
colors, changing 19
Cottage Tea Cozy 84–87
Crochet Edge Cards and Tags 27, 116–121
Crochet Edge Frames 57–59
Crochet Hook Organizer 66–71
crochet hooks 123
Crochet Latte 104–106

D

Diana Camera Purse 26, 88–90
Diana Camera Purse fabric lining 26
double crochet 16

E

embroidery 20–21, 22, 79–83, 104–106, 52–56
"Enjoy" Place Setting Placemat 79–83

F

fastening off 19
foundation chain 14
French knot 22

G

Gift Boxes 96–103
glossary 122
Granny Square Infinity Cowl 30–33

H

half double crochet 17
Heart Pocket Apron 72–75
"Home Cozy Home" Pillow Case 52–56
home décor
    Cottage Tea Cozy 84–87
    Crochet Edge Frames 57–59
    "Home Cozy Home" Pillow Case 52–56
    Ombré Baskets in Three Sizes 62–65
Party Hat Garland 110–115
Snow Cone Garland 113–115
Teacup Coasters 76–78

M

materials 10

O

Ombré Baskets in Three Sizes 62–65

P

Party Hat Garland 110–112

R

resources 125

S

Scallop Stripe Cowl 48–49
single crochet 15
slip knot 13
slip stitch 19
Snow Cone Garland 113–115
Stripe Bow Clutch 38–41
Sweater Makeover 42–44

T

Tablet Case 25, 91–93
Tablet Case lining 25
Teacup Coasters 76–78
tools 10
treble crochet 18

W

weaving in ends 19

Y

Yarn Bag Makeover 60–61
yarn weights, standard 123

Z

zipper, sewing on 23